The Borderline Patient

COMMENTARY

The increased use of the term "borderline" and the many names applied to a large area of clinical uncertainty in psychiatric diagnosis raises several important questions: Does it represent a modern tendency toward diagnostic vagueness? Is there a real increase in the incidence of the syndrome? Or is there a spreading recognition of a new clinical entity?

This revised and expanded edition of the now classic work, *The Borderline Syndrome*, presents the results of a lengthy systematic research program on the "borderline syndrome"—a widely used but ill-defined and little-understood category. From an intensive study of hospitalized patients characterized as "borderline," detailed follow-ups after their discharge, and investigations of their families, the authors have sought to understand this elusive entity and to define its characteristics in process or ego-functions terms.

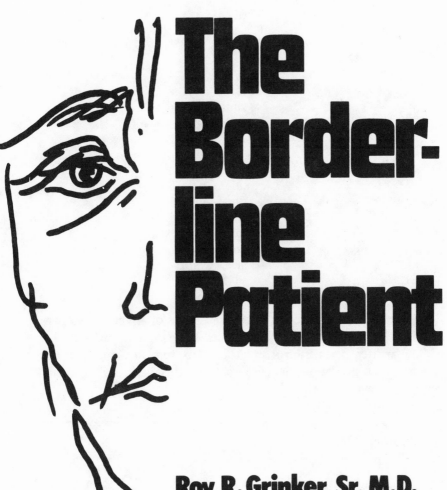

The Border-line Patient

Roy R. Grinker, Sr. M.D.
and
Beatrice Werble Ph.D.

New York • Jason Aronson • London

Preface

In 1968 we published *The Borderline Syndrome*, in which we reported hospitalized borderline patients. Using a detailed analysis of daily behaviors as an index of their ego-functions, we attempted (1) to understand the characteristics of this vague nosological entity (previously designated by a number of labels), (2) to define the group as a whole, and (3) to determine its subgroups.

Today psychiatrists are concerned more with the life history of describable entities than with internal dynamics and individual patients regardless of diagnosis. If clinical psychiatry is a science it must be based on adequate observation, description, diagnosis, and classification.

In *The Borderline Syndrome* we devised a research method suitable for the clarification of hitherto unclear syndromes, using a theory of ego psychology and a complicated statistical analysis. Thus we were able to identify the borderline group as a whole and to describe its subgroups. Unfortunately these characteristics are not easily extrapolated to the behaviors of individual patients, and the psychiatric clinician has often been confused and unable to use our research findings for diagnosis with any degree of confidence.

The present book is essentially an attempt to clarify for the clinical psychiatrist what the borderline patient is and what he is not. We have therefore entitled it *The Borderline Patient*. It does not repeat the assumptions, methods, and statistics of the original work, which is available to investigators; instead it emphasizes the clinical manifestations of the borderline syndrome and how it is differentiated from other entities. To follow this clinical approach we have used the applicable clinical cases reported earlier and added others which were part of a current research program that includes family data, psychological test material, and some follow-up studies using descriptive methods, profiles, and contrasting diagnoses.

Our first book—and the research on which it was based—took eight years of work. On its publication we acknowledged the help of some 105 persons, including administrators, residents, nurses, social workers, activities workers, and research assistants. As *The Borderline Patient* includes material from the earlier monograph, we repeat with gratitude our acknowledgment of their efforts.

In addition we would like to thank those who helped with the current work: Dr. Edward Wolpert and the members of our Schizophrenic Research Program (from which our new cases have been drawn), including Drs. Philip Holzman, Martin Harrow, Doris Gruenewald, Mary Rootes, Don Schwartz, Froma Walsh, Marion Levin, and Judy Beck. We regret that Dr. Robert C. Drye was unable to continue his participation.

Contents

Chapter 1
This Vague Entity

From the literature on the borderline we are convinced that there is scarcely a general understanding of the term and no consensus on differentiating criteria that would lead to accurate, consistent, and reliable diagnoses. There are few clinical descriptive or psychoanalytic reports based on supportive data, and there are only confused dynamic formulations. Clinicians generally agree that borderline patients appear clinically unclear and that they occupy an area in psychopathology where accurate diagnosis is difficult. Beyond this small island of common ground, varying assumptions are made.

To summarize the clinical positions: some say there is no such thing as borderlines, that they are schizophrenics; others say that the borderline may be a state of transition from neurosis to psychosis; finally, others believe that a borderline condition is relatively stable personality disturbance with psychotic, neurotic, and healthy ego-functions present simultaneously, and that the range of symptoms includes those characteristic of an extensive spectrum from neurotic to

psychotic. Whichever of the last two positions is taken, there is
agreement that among these patients certain ego-functions
are rather severely impaired (Knight 1953).

This then is the problem, as distilled from experience with
patients who were unclearly defined and usually unsuccess-
fully treated. Is the term *borderline* a wastebasket into which
all puzzling cases are dumped? Are there clinical, dynamic, or
other characteristics which could define them as members of a
single nosological category? And are there multiple subcategories?

Why Diagnosis?

Is classification within the nosological systems in psychiatry important or isn't it? This is a debate that has generated
considerable heat in the past. For those who consider
psychiatry a part of medicine, the traditional formula of
history taking and examination, diagnosis, and then treatment is still unquestioned. When psychoanalytic psychiatry
became dominant in the United States and the methods of
observation and description were demoted, diagnosis was at
first considered an unimportant medical orthodoxy only
possible—if at all necessary—during treatment; later, when it
came to be seen as a pejorative labeling of persons for life, the
credo became: "It is not the diagnosis but *this* patient's
problems in living that are my concern." Indeed some went so
far as to call mental illness a myth. All denied the adage
"naming is knowing" (Bentley 1950). Stengel assessed the
situation as of 1959:

Psychiatry has made considerable strides during the past three
decades. There has been great therapeutic activity and an
enormous intensification of research work. Medical men, public
authorities, and the community at large have become alive to
the magnitude of the problems of mental disorders. Conditions
for a concerted attack on mental ill health ought, therefore, to be
highly propitious at the present time. Yet, in many respects,

psychiatrists find themselves ill-prepared to meet the challenge. This is partly due to the incomplete integration of the various approaches to the study of mental illness, though there are signs that this process has been gaining momentum of late. A more serious obstacle to progress in psychiatry is difficulty of communication. Everybody who has followed the literature and listened to discussions concerning mental illness soon discovers that psychiatrists, even those apparently sharing the same basic orientation, often do not speak the same language. They either use different terms for the same concepts, or the same term for different concepts, usually without being aware of it. It is sometimes argued that this is inevitable in the present state of psychiatric knowledge, but it is doubtful whether this is a valid excuse.

The lack of a common classification of mental disorders has defeated attempts at comparing psychiatric observations and the results of treatments undertaken in various countries or even in various centers of the same country. Possibly, if greater attention had been paid to these difficulties, there might be a greater measure of agreement about the value of specific treatments than exists today. Another field in which the lack of a common language threatens to defeat the purpose of much valuable effort is that of experimental psychiatry where research has been very active of late. In recent years the epidemiological approach has been used in the study of mental disorders to an increasing degree. To be fruitfully employed on a broad front it requires a common basic terminology and classification. There is a real danger that the lack of such a vehicle of communication will lead to confusion and to a waste of previous resources. [Stengel 1959]

More recently, one of the authors (Grinker 1964) wrote:

Psychiatry in its role as a branch of medicine or as an applied science is concerned with diagnosis and various forms of therapy. This field is and has been extremely confused ever since man began to function as a medicine-man healer. It is only lately that scientific methods have been applied in an attempt to

understand the rationale, methods and results of psychotherapy. If we dodge the issue that there are categories of mental
disturbances with specific course, and prognosis, we have no
science. There can be no scientific therapy without clinical
categories as guidelines to facilitate the study of the life-history
of specific disturbances, their spontaneous course and the
interrelationships among causative factors. Studies of the
various treatments for mentally ill patients require the
establishing of diagnostic categories, defining the methods
applicable to each and developing criteria for results.

    Glover (1932) approached the problem of classification from
the psychoanalytic point of view, finding it a "matted
complexity," especially the complicated transitional forms
which certainly include the borderline. He stated that
psychiatric classifications based on clinical description are
unsatisfactory because, as end products, they do not include
unconscious processes and genetic (developmental) elements.
He believed there was room for new syndromes achieved by
"openness" for which a combination of descriptive words with
genetic understanding would be necessary to aid differential
diagnosis and refine prognosis. Glover added that there
should be an intelligible relation between the phenomena of
psychiatry and the psychological phenomena (behavior) of
everyday life. The function of psychological adaptation is
thus a boundary process between perceptual organization and
drive processes as subserved by an ego which defines a sense
of reality. For Glover the term *borderline* was as unsatisfactory as *prepsychotic*, because in the phases of development there
is a normal madness and everyone is a larval psychotic.

    Is classification and the current nosology the true bible of
modern psychiatry or does it as a rigid and strict codifier
hinder deeper understanding? Such a pseudoquestion has no
answer but "both" (Menninger 1963). No science can exist
without a foundation of description and classification of its
"what," its object of study. Nor can it develop beyond a
primitive state without transcending the purely descriptive,

without answering the dynamic etiological question "how," which deals with process, and the question "why," which considers purpose and meaning.

When we published our research monograph on the borderline in 1968 after eight years of work observing, describing, rating, and statistical analysis, we were satisfied we had described a separate entity with four subtypes. But research that isolates a syndrome sacrifices detailed protocols of individual patients. This we attempted to rectify by describing in detail a few individual patients. Apparently these examples were too few or insufficiently clear, because clinicians still had difficulty diagnosing their patients.

Two major mistakes are constantly reported at meetings and in publications. The first is the use of the term *borderline schizophrenia*. Our work and that of others indicate that the schizophrenias exist as syndromes characterized by specific behaviors, affects, and thought disorders. A person is either schizophrenic or not. In other words, schizophrenia is not latent or borderline. Furthermore *schizophrenia* is not equivalent to *psychosis*. The latter term applies to schizophrenics who have disintegrated, to some manic-depressives, and to psychoses related to toxins, infections, trauma, cerebral arteriosclerosis, senility, and so forth. A person may be close to a psychotic break, but his essential problem is not the final psychotic disintegration that occurs in about 40 percent of the pseudoneurotic schizophrenias described by Hoch and Polatin (1949).

The second mistake is that the diagnosis of borderline schizophrenia is based on a series of core phenomena consisting of developmental distortions of ego-functions. These are: anger as the main or only affect, a defect in attaining and maintaining affectional relationships, absence of adequate self-identity, and depressive loneliness. Our four subtypes deal with such defects in a variety of ways but these defenses, substitutions, and adaptations do not constitute the borderline and are no different from those seen in a variety of other psychiatric disturbances. These secondary neurotic and

behavioral symptoms include fantasy, religious preoccupation, drug addiction and abuse, alcoholism, anorexia or
obesity, suicide attempts, and a wide variety of other
symptoms overlaying the essence of the borderline. This will
be demonstrated in our detailed case histories.

Chapter 2
Views of the Borderline Syndrome

Surveying what has been written on the subject of the borderline is extraordinarily difficult. The literature on any vague clinical entity of course presents problems, but these are especially knotty when one diagnostic term has been applied to a variety of symptoms and syndromes. Whatever the term *borderline* means specifically, it implies a variable combination of neurotic and psychotic symptoms. Still, this is true of every psychiatric syndrome and of phases of development succeeded by states of relative health.

A survey of the literature on the borderline syndrome points up the need for investigating the increasing use of a clinical diagnosis with no generally accepted meaning. We have therefore tried to determine how the clinical syndrome or gestalt has been viewed rather than to describe specific symptoms. Certainly this focus should precede attempts to define the developmental factors, dynamic patterns, clinical courses, and end results, as well as the differential diagnosis. We shall attempt to cite briefly descriptions and dynamic formulations of the borderline when the term is used or implied, avoiding quotation from author to author, of which there are many.

The Early Use
of Borderline in Psychiatry

An overview of the literature could extend to antiquity and
we would probably find our predecessors at least somewhat
aware of the problems puzzling us today. We could undertake
to interpret their generalized statements to apply to our
current concepts, but the difficulty is compounded when such
nontechnical terms as *borderline* or *borderland* are employed
to denote similarity to schizophrenia, an entity accounting for
volumes of scientific literature. We choose, therefore, to
restrict ourselves to the era of modern psychiatry.

We have uncovered such statements as "the borderland of
insanity is occupied by many persons who pass their whole
life near that line, sometimes on one side, sometimes on the
other" by Hughes (1884), or a description of patients "in the
twilight of right reason and despair" by Rosse (1890). Among
the conditions considered in this borderland were severe
obsessions, compulsions, phobias, hysteria, and neurasthe-
nia. When Kraepelin (1912) developed his first psychiatric
classification, the borderline was drawn between the neuroses
and the schizophrenias. Bleuler (1955), however, did not use
the term *borderline* but extended the concept of latent
schizophrenia to include character anomalies occurring
before the onset of schizophrenic psychosis.

Jones (1918) stated that dementia praecox has nothing to do
with neuroses: "The borderland has already been crossed."
Others thought that a variety of hysterical or obsessive
symptoms could be considered incipient dementia praecox.
Clark (1919) described periodic depression and mild dementia
praecox as borderland states. A number of other papers put
forth the opinion that borderline meant cases of mental illness
which could not be considered insanity, yet were neither
normal nor neurotic.

In general the borderline or borderland designation
indicated diagnostic difficulties at a time when insanity
meant commitability and loss of legal responsibility. Many
seriously troubled patients to whom the current nosology was

not applicable could manage to live outside an institution. Were they latent or incipient schizophrenics, borderline, or what? Was it possible that a combination of psychotic and psychoneurotic components could exist in the same case, or that a psychoneurosis could mask a psychosis? These and other similar questions troubled psychiatrists who were seriously and often entirely concerned with diagnosis and classification.

Modern Clinical Descriptions

Perhaps we can say that this era began when Glover (1932) wrote: "I find the term *borderline* or *prepsychotic* as generally used unsatisfactory. If a psychotic mechanism is present at all, it should be given a definite label." Glover believed that the terms *transitional* or *potential* clinical psychosis should be retained because they, unlike borderline, dovetail with the psychoanalytic concept of regression.

The increasing number of patients who fit into neither the psychoneurotic nor the psychotic groups and who were not amenable to psychoanalytic therapy led Stern (1938) to define the borderline as a group of neuroses, thereby making them diagnostically respectable. His patients, as a result of deficient maternal affection, suffered severe narcissistic damage leading to hypersensitivity, defects in self-esteem, rigidity of personality as defense against anxiety, and "psychic bleeding" or paralysis—these, rather than active reactions. Their insecurities led to intense anxiety at disapproval, which also interfered with psychotherapy because all interpretations were considered criticisms.

Stern wrote:

A certain vagueness is at present unavoidable because the material which this group offers for study runs so clearly in two directions, namely, toward the psychotic and the psychoneurotic. Much more time and investigation are necessary to evaluate the rather obscure phenomena these patients present. That they form a group by themselves, which one can designate as borderline, is a justifiable assumption.

Knight (1954) presented a definitive statement of the term. In summary, he wrote that the term *borderline* has achieved almost no official status in psychiatric nomenclature, and conveys no diagnostic illumination of a case other than the implication that the patient is quite sick but not definitely psychotic. In textbooks where the term appears, it is applied to cases in which the decision as to whether the patient in question is neurotic or psychotic is difficult, phenomena related to both conditions being observed. (Compare our selection criteria for patients in the study.)

These patients have frequently been diagnosed as having psychoneuroses of severe degree. Most often, they have been called severe obsessive-compulsive cases; sometimes an intractable phobia has been the outstanding symptom. Occasionally an apparent major hysterical symptom or an anorexia nervosa dominates the clinical picture, and at times it is a question of the degree of depression, the extent and malignancy of paranoid trends, or the severity of a character disorder. All these diagnoses refer to peripheral symptoms.

Knight noted that structured interviews are deceptive because under conventional circumstances these patients behave adequately. Fenichel (1945) added that the borderline patient appears normal as long as security prevails. Careful attention to details, however, enables the psychiatrist to detect suspiciousness, peculiarities and contamination in thinking, and lack of concern about realities. There are few clues to possible precipitating factors.

Schmideberg (1959) described the borderline as a syndrome blending normality, neuroses, psychoses, and psychopathy in a relatively stable lifelong pattern. *Differentiation is made not from the specific symptoms but by severe personality disturbances involving every aspect of living.* Borderline patients have difficulty in feeling genuine emotions in work and study. They are nonsocial, often paranoid and aggressive.

These patients are unhappy but not depressed, are inconsistent, holding contrasting attitudes, and often reveal poor observations of reality resulting in faulty judgments. They have difficulty in assuming responsibility and frequently utilize the defensive mechanism of denial. According to Schmideberg, weak object relations are associated with hostile acting-out behavior, in an attempt to break through insensitivity, and with low tolerance for frustration. They acquire little real knowledge, tend to sponge on their families and drift through life.

Schmideberg states that one reason why the borderline should be regarded as a clinical entity is that the patient, as a rule, remains substantially the same throughout his life. He is "stable in his instability" and often even keeps his pattern of peculiarity constant. Parkin (1966) also states that the borderline is a stable state of transition in which the neurosis is a defense against psychosis. As the borderline condition rarely ushers in schizophrenia, it should not be regarded as a prepsychotic condition (a diagnosis usually made ex post facto), as latent schizophrenia, or as pseudoneurotic schizophrenia. While some schizophrenics in remission may resemble borderlines, the latter are different because they have not been and are not likely to become schizophrenics. The borderline concept should also be distinguished from that of psychotic episodes, temporary or partial schizophrenic reactions to stress. *The characteristic features of the borderline patient are not his symptoms.* He certainly lacks the more obvious psychotic ones: delusions, far-reaching disorganizations or regressions, manic elation, or melancholic depression. Though he is often suspicious and collects grievances, he has no true paranoid symptoms, nor has he the dramatic symptoms of the hysteric or the obsessional. Depression, anxiety, and other painful feelings may accompany any disorder and are experienced even by normal people under stress; borderlines as well often suffer from them. But more interesting is their frequent lack of normal feelings.

According to Eisenstein (1952), borderline patients are

made anxious by aloofness of manner in others yet are suspicious of warmth. They are plagued by negative feelings. Knight pointed out that, despite severe damage, patients' ego-functions, adaptating to the demands of the environment for conventional behavior, are adequate, superficial object relations are intact, and habitual performances are unimpaired. Others have pointed out that in a well-structured situation borderlines conform, although in a somewhat eccentric, whimsical, or queer fashion. In an unstructured situation they may display a wide variety of confusions, indicating the essential pathology of the ego-functions.

In the literature there are many individual case reports from which are drawn extensive conclusions which seem to have influenced subsequent reports. Under the auspices of the Postgraduate Psychoanalytic Seminar at the Chicago Psychoanalytic Institute, first the late Albrecht Meyer and then Stanford Gamm held monthly meetings with sixteen psychoanalysts to discuss their pooled borderline cases in various forms of treatment. They state:

The clinical characteristics of the borderline patient include low self-esteem, extreme sensitivity to criticism and rejection, suspiciousness and distrust, and extreme fearfulness. They are very afraid of aggression, in themselves and others, of loving and being close, of responsibility, and of change in general. Their interpersonal relationships tend to be tenuous and tentative, and their reality orientation is often deficient. They use denial and projection to a much greater extent than the neurotic person. Their intense longing for approval and closeness, and their simultaneous fear of it leads to marked feelings of loneliness and emptiness, in the extreme to utter void and despair.

These cases distribute themselves along a spectrum of increasing disturbance from the more severe psychoneurotic to the most disturbed "borderline" case, closely resembling the overt psychotic. At the healthier end of the spectrum are the narcissistic character neuroses with strong narcissistic defenses, giving them an appearance, more or less, of normality. They come to analysis only after serious crises in their lives have cracked their armor. This group also includes successful narcissists whose defenses succumb only to old age or retirement. In the center of the spectrum are the bulk of cases—less stable, less successful, more erratic, more actively disturbed. They tend to act out more, trying to fill up their emptiness with alcohol, excessive sexual indulgence, or any other kind of excitement. But they do manage to preserve considerable successful adaptation. Closest to the psychotics are the most disturbed patients, who show considerable paranoid ideation, marked feelings of void, very tenuous object relations, and the most marginal adjustment. In spite of their serious pathology, what seems to characterize the bulk of borderline patients is their resistance to psychotic illness.

Psychodynamic Formulations

Under this heading most of the literature on the borderline can be found. Unfortunately the reports are repetitive, discursive, and not well documented by empirical reference. Knight (1953) wrote:

We conceptualize the borderline case as one in which normal ego-functions of secondary-process thinking, integration, realistic planning, adaptation to the environment, maintenance of object relationships, and defenses against primitive unconscious impulses are severely weakened. As a result of various combinations of the factors of constitutional tendencies, predisposition based on traumatic events and disturbed human relationships, and more recent precipitating stress, the ego of the borderline patient is laboring badly. Some ego-functions have been severely impaired—especially, in most cases, integration, concept formation, judgment, realistic planning, and defending against eruption into conscious thinking of id impulses and their fantasy elaborations. Other ego-functions, such as conventional (but superficial) adaptation to the environment and superficial maintenance of object relationships may exhibit varying degrees of intactness. And still others, such as memory, calculation, and certain habitual performances may seem unimpaired. Also, the clinical picture may be dominated by hysterical, phobic, obsessive-compulsive, or psychosomatic symptoms, to which neurotic disabilities and distress the patient attributes his inability to carry on the usual ego-functions.

It is generally accepted that the ego or integrating functions of the borderline are severely damaged as a result of deep narcissistic injuries early in life. Eisenstein (1952) points out that borderline patients tend to act out by running away, becoming promiscuous, or using drugs to excess. There is anxiety over coldness or aloofness in others and suspiciousness of their warmth or attempts at closeness. In moving toward closeness they seem to fear loss of differentiation or being "swallowed up" by another and, according to Fried (1956), react with hostility and detachment.

Waelder (1960) ascribes the feeling of emptiness in the borderline as the basis of an attempt to appropriate from others, or of a feeling of danger of being engulfed by others. Some try to borrow from others, become satellites of another, merge with a host, or lie skin to skin. Others attempt to fill up with knowledge or experience.

Although the borderline knows himself as an object, he often acts his role. He needs to experience excitation but fears being overwhelmed by it. As Modell (1963) states: "It is the porcupine's dilemma; to sleep as close to his fellows to get the needed warmth from their bodies, yet to maintain sufficient distance to avoid being stuck by their quills." The cause of the borderline's early repression of large segments of his affective resources is not easily determined. These patients often come from intelligent, educated, and involved parents of relatively high socioeconomic levels.

Modell points out that schizophrenia is a final common

pathway of a variety of pathological conditions. The borderline, however, is not an incipient or early schizophrenic,
although among the wide variety of borderline symptom-
complexes are withdrawal, depression, and schizoid personalities. Although his object relations are primitive, the borderline is nevertheless able to maintain some ties with other
people. Modell, among others, thinks the borderline designation indicates a structural diagnosis rather than a syndrome
with specific symptoms. Among the qualities of the borderline
he includes: (1) subtle disorder in sense of reality; (2) strained
quality of identifications and sense of identity; (3) relations
based on primary identification instead of on love, with
identity borrowed from the partner; (4) primitive destructive
fantasies; (5) temporary and limited regressions; and (6) wish
for omnipotent protectors and enormous dependence on
external objects, but accompanied by intense fear of closeness.
On the positive side the borderline is relatively stable and does
not develop overt schizophrenic breakdowns. According to
Modell, the borderline is an example of developmental arrest
due to deficient mothering.

Borderline in Children

Ekstein and Wallerstein (1954) write:

Time and again the child begins the therapy hour with
conversation or play wholly suited to his chronological age, so
the clinical observer may reasonably be ready to conjecture the
presence of a relatively intact ego, well able to use and sustain
the demands and vicissitudes of classical child therapy and
analysis. Yet suddenly and without clearly perceptible stimulus,
a dramatic shift may occur, the neurotic defenses crumble
precipitously and the archaic mechanisms of the primary
process and the psychotic defenses erupt into view. Then they
recede just as rapidly and the neurotic defenses or perhaps more
accurately the pseudo-neurotic defenses reappear.

Rosenfeld and Sprince (1963) report pooled cases of a group working with borderline children to demonstrate that the interpreted dynamics even in the early years of life are no different from those of adults. These children have a precarious maintenance of object cathexis, easily retreating into primary identifications (mimicry). Their disturbance is principally in the perceptive and integrative abilities of the ego to select and inhibit stimuli. Considerable anxiety is aroused by primitive fears of disintegration. Most such children are uncertain about their sexual identity and reveal a discrepancy in their sexual and aggressive drives. Among the clinical derivatives of the lack of pleasurable early experiences and the resultant lack of ego stability are (1) hypersensitivity to the environment, (2) disintegration under stress, (3) inability to accept frustration, (4) aggression toward people to whom they are attached, and (5) difficulty in sorting out the importance of several possible choices of behavior.

Is There a Borderline at All?

Bychowski (1957) uses the term *latent schizophrenia* instead of *borderline*, as did Federn (1952) following Bleuler (1950), who spoke of latent schizophrenia as a group of all sorts of deviant personalities in which are concealed all the symptoms and combinations of symptoms observable in the manifest types of the disease. Bychowski's clinical descriptions of the borderline, in comparison with those outlined by others, do not fit into this category, but are indeed characteristic of the manifest schizophrenias.

The term *pseudoneurotic schizophrenia* was coined by Hoch and Polatin (1949). In a letter dated February 7, 1963 Hoch stated:

In the paper "The Diagnosis of Pseudoneurotic Schizophrenia," you will find a discussion which would indicate why I do not feel that pseudoneurotic schizophrenia is synonymous with the borderline concept. To put it very plainly an ambulatory schizo-phrenic is a schizophrenic in any category who is not sufficiently ill or whose socioeconomic condition is such that he does not have to be hospitalized. Pseudoneurotic schizophrenia is a subentity of schizophrenia similar to the catatonic or paranoid states, and finally I believe borderline should be dropped completely because I do not know what borders on what. Furthermore, I do not believe that a neurotic becomes schizophrenic and vice versa. I think there are two different processes involved if one considers it purely from the point of view of ego-function or ego control. [1963; see also Hoch 1972]

Hoch and Cattell (1959) vigorously opposed the borderline or latent schizophrenic terms as logically untenable. Here, however, the more specific details of their "pseudoneurotic" schizophrenias indicate that these patients are schizophrenic and not what other clinicians have called borderline.

Frosch (1964) has suggested that the concept of psychotic character be substituted for that of borderline as well as ambulatory schizophrenia, pseudoneurotic schizophrenia, pseudopathic schizophrenia, schizophrenia without psy-choses, latent psychoses, larval psychoses, "as if" character, and neurotic ego distortion. This presupposes that symptoms or clusters of symptoms are not suitable for classification. Instead he has reference to a syndrome characterized by ego-functions in their relationships to reality, other objects, and other psychic structures. The psychotic character differs from psychosis as follows: (1) relative preservation of capacity to test reality; (2) relatively higher level of object relations but still on an infantile level; (3) capacity for reversibility of regression, giving transience to the appearance of psychotic symptoms; and (4) reality adaptation. The psychotic charac-ter reveals a wide range of clinical manifestations, all of which are subsumed under one syndrome characterized in essence by transient perceptual distortions, identification, depersonalization, and regressions.

Helene Deutsch (1942) described a syndrome she called the

"as if" personality disorder; it is evidenced in those rare individuals whose relationships are based on mimicry or imitation of others. Thirty years later two of her treated patients who had been successful in their careers were still utilizing the same method in relationships. Subsequent to Deutsch's presentation the "as if" syndrome was broadened to include the syndrome now called the borderline.

Deutsch's patients apparently had not regressed but were fixed at an early infantile level of development at which there was still a primitive stage of object relations, with little consistency, poor superego development, primary processes of identification, lack of sense of identity, poverty of affect, and lack of insight. These patients were sufficiently able to test reality to prevent the development of psychosis (Weiss 1966).

We attempted to sample the opinions of contemporary local psychiatric practitioners on our staff who had experience in diagnosing and treating what they termed borderline patients. Because opinions were so uncrystallized, only 10 percent of over one hundred psychiatrists responded. Among the respondents there was no single stereotype. In fact the divergence of "opinions" reflected the findings of our overview of the literature. Metapsychological pronouncements, observations, interpretations, and inferences were presented with great semantic confusion. We concluded, that the diagnosis of borderline represented at best a label for uncertainty and the search for a niche in which to place many varieties of human distress.

The reader is probably astonished at the paucity of clinical observations and descriptions up to 1968 and perhaps somewhat curious that the main body of writing stems rather from psychoanalysts than from general psychiatrists. And it is indeed surprising that this clinical syndrome, increasingly diagnosed in office practice and in psychiatric clinics, has not been the subject of systematic empirical research.

The dynamic formulations are somewhat repetitive, and the arguments regarding nuances of meaning are characteristic of much modern psychoanalytic discussion, in that definitions and semantic clarity are missing. For example, one contributor to a panel thought that there existed a "pseudo-as-if" character. Furthermore, the dynamic speculators rarely revealed the sources of the clinical data about which they were talking or writing, the number of patients they had observed, or the techniques employed. Apparently the growing attention paid the borderline by psychoanalysts is indicative of the increasing numbers of these patients seen in their private practices.

Despite these limitations, the clinical descriptions and formulations do attain a general consensus, and the reader surely can grasp the currently accepted gestalt of the borderline. True, there are some who deny that the concept has heuristic value or empirical validity. They prefer to include the borderline among the latent, incipient, ambulatory, or transitional schizophrenics. Yet they fail to identify their patients or to discuss the absence of disturbances of associations or other cognitive functions characteristic of schizophrenia. It is striking as well that the data concerning the borderline syndrome are markedly similar regardless of patients' ages and within a wide socioeconomic range.

The general consensus, without repeating the details, is that the borderline is not a regressive process but a developmental defect overlaid by wide varieties of adaptive and defensive neurotic behavior. The defect is fundamentally a deformity or distortion of ego-functions. The etiological factors for this arrest of development are not known, and the age of phase represented by the fixation has not been delineated.

The so-called structural defect of the ego produces a deficiency in the processes of identifications; these are maintained at the infantile level of mimicry and do not reach the secondary level characterized by confidence, independence, and the development of regulatory structures. Affectionate relations are sought but feared; loneliness is sometimes defended against by participating with others on an "as if" level; structured situations are more comfortable than the uncertainty of change; and the sense of identity is woefully weak.

It is generally agreed that specific symptoms, most of them neurotic, do not characterize the borderline, nor do minor, transient psychotic withdrawals. The essential quality of the borderline is the defect or distortion of ego-functions. Indeed, our review of the literature points clearly to the need for systematic research into the ego-functions of the borderline.

By 1968 the term *borderline* had not yet reached the *Diagnostic and Statistical Manual* of the American Psychiatric Association, although it is proposed for DSM III, nor today, eight years later, can the term be found either in the formal terminology of the American Medical Association or in *International Classifications of Psychiatric Disorders*. The diagnosis *borderline*, despite the absence of consensus regarding the meaning of the term, is widely used in the United States and is especially fashionable and prevalent in some eastern sections of the country that boast of sophisticated practice in psychiatry. Because of the conflicting views in the literature regarding the meaning of the term, the diagnosis of borderline is likely to be made on an idiosyncratic basis, that is, in terms of what is compatible with the internal program of the clinician rather than with validated or reliable criteria.

Several timely attempts to bring order into this chaotic state have in recent years been undertaken. Gunderson and Singer (1975) reviewed the descriptive literature on borderline patients and concluded that the accounts vary, depending on who is describing the patients, in what context, how the samples are selected, and what data are collected. Based on their review of the literature, these authors describe six features for diagnosing borderline patients during an initial interview: (1) the presence of intense affect usually depressive or hostile (in agreement with Grinker et al.), (2) a history of impulsive behavior, (3) a certain social adaptiveness, (4) brief psychotic experiences, (5) loose thinking in unstructured situations, and (6) relationships that vacillate between superficiality and intense dependency.

Gunderson and Singer's article also contained a useful review of the psychological test literature. Generally, agreement prevails that the borderline demonstrates ordinary reasoning and responses to such structured tests as the

Wechsler Adult Intelligence Scale (WAIS), but that less structured tests such as the Rorschach reveal deviant thought and communication processes. The authors state that most articles on which this conclusion is based are impressionistic, as was noted of the clinical literature. Many methodological issues require attention before this broadly held viewpoint can be accepted.

These authors add the cogent point that the initial selection criteria used both by Hoch and Cattell and by Grinker et al. influenced the conclusions reached about borderline patients. Gunderson and Singer liken the problem to packing a suitcase and then being surprised to find what is in it when it is opened. The selection of samples for research in clinical psychiatry by unbiased means is a monotonously repetitive methodological problem to which sampling experts may someday profitably contribute.

We do not deny that sampling problems are difficult, with variations in different parts of the country, different nations, different cultures, and different investigative biases. Our section on selection of patients for study is repeated here from *The Borderline Syndrome* because it focused on attempts to choose nonschizophrenic, non-brain-damaged individuals in a group difficult to diagnose. Our "suitcase was packed" with a variety of syndromes preparatory for an eight-year research journey. Our suitcase was stuffed with a heterogeneous sample but when unpacked at journey's end revealed to our surprise four orderly groupings or subtypes.

Selection of Patients for Study

The chief of the Reese psychiatric unit, Dr. Theodore Reid, Jr., was asked to admit as many nondiagnosable patients as possible, which meant patients who definitely were not overtly schizophrenic. In retrospect, he interpreted our general criteria along the following lines:

1. Young adult with repeated short-term hospitalizations but with good psychological functioning in the intervals

2. Florid attention-provoking histrionic episodes preceding hospitalization
3. Quite accessible during the diagnostic interview or rapidly becoming so
4. Intellectual contact possible and cognitive functions intact
5. Associations appropriate
6. No systematized delusions, hallucinations, or paranoid systems
7. An ego-alien quality to any transient psychoticlike behavior

Excluded from the study were patients who:

1. Gave evidence of damage from alcohol or drugs
2. Suffered from degenerative diseases
3. Were beyond middle years
5. Had experienced a discernible loss of memory from shock therapy

Thus patients whose ego-functioning might be impaired for physical or organic reasons were excluded.

Although these criteria appear rather loose, from the point of view of the research they were a very satisfactory basis for referral. The purpose of the study, which was the development of diagnostic typologies within an ego-functions framework, required that we identify a range of behavior with considerable variety. Had we attempted a tighter definition we would have invalidated our purpose.

The syndrome may be manifested at times by behavior that seems sufficiently psychotic to warrant admission to a psychiatric receiving hospital. Many of our patients were procured for transfer to our unit from the Psychopathic Hospital. Yet on admission, their psychotic behavior hardly ever appeared or reappeared because our structured milieu furnished fewer tests of ability to cope with the world. That the patients understood the stresses presented them on the outside world is evidenced by their later reluctance to leave the security of our hospital.

In a further effort to establish the degree to which borderline patients form a category distinct from the schizophrenic,

TO _____

DATE _____

WHILE YOU WERE OUT

M _____

OF _____

PHONE _____

TELEPHONED		PLEASE CALL	
CALLED TO SEE YOU		WILL CALL AGAIN	
WANTS TO SEE YOU		RET'D YOUR CALL	

MESSAGE _____

_____

_____

_____

_____

Gunderson, Carpenter, and Strauss (1975) undertook a comparative study. Specifically, they examined matched groups of borderline and schizophrenic patients in terms of psychotic symptoms, dissociative experiences, affective symptoms, prognostic scores, and outcomes at two-year follow-up. The investigators laudably aimed to provide a replicable method of sample selection and standardized evaluating procedures for a systematic follow-up. This investigation was carried out using data collected from the 142 patients evaluated in the Washington, D.C. area, which comprised the U.S. subsample of the International Pilot Study of Schizophrenia. Patients were drawn for study from a cohort of recent admissions to three psychiatric hospitals in Maryland. The admitted patients were screened for (1) age between fifteen and forty-five, (2) no evidence of organic, drug-related, or alcoholic disorders, (3) not hospitalized for more than two out of the previous five years, (4) no evidence of continuous psychosis for longer than three years, and (5) suggestive evidence on admission of psychotic symptoms, such as hallucinations, delusions, thinking disorder, bizarre behavior, or severe withdrawal. The 142 patients who met these screening criteria included a relatively acutely ill group of patients with a broad spectrum of severe psychiatric problems.

To select a group of borderline patients from this pool, two criteria were used: (1) All patients were excluded who had severe or continuous psychotic symptoms (including hallucinations, delusions, thinking disorders, and bizarre behavior). The only patients exempted were those given the clinical diagnosis of borderline by the interviewing psychiatrist. Forty-two patients remained in the sample after this initial exclusion process. (2) All subjects with a diagnosis (considered certain) other than borderline were excluded. A final sample of twenty-four borderline patients remained for study.

To obtain a comparison group of schizophrenic patients, those who met all of the following criteria were selected from the original pool of 142: (1) a clinical diagnosis of certain schizophrenia, (2) one or more of Schneider's first-rank symptoms, and (3) the presence of six or more of the twelve symptoms that best discriminate schizophrenia. These strict criteria ensured the selection of patients who were as well defined and as definitely schizophrenic as possible by current diagnostic standards. This matching process left a total sample of twenty-nine schizophrenic patients.

The borderline and schizophrenic patients were compared in terms of their symptoms, prognostic scores, and outcome results. The authors were dismayed by the finding that, despite their discrepant symptom pictures, borderline and schizophrenic patients had remarkably similar prognostic and outcome characteristics—a finding we would strenuously dispute. They go on to suggest that these prognostic and outcome similarities reflect basic underlying similarities between the two samples, and suggest finally that the treatment given both groups may have been more helpful to the schizophrenics than to the borderlines—a suggestion not borne out in our experience. Gunderson et al. used selection criteria that screened out patients hospitalized for more than two out of the previous five years and no evidence of continuous psychosis for longer than three years. Since these criteria slant selection of patients to those with accurate episodes, similar prognosis and outcome characteristics after two years should come as no surprise. There are many ways to pack a suitcase, even when the suitcase contains a replicable matched sample. Also at issue in accounting for the findings of similar prognosis and outcome is the question of the validity of relying on an arbitrarily drawn-up symptom profile, based on the review of the literature, as criteria defining the borderline.

Kernberg (1967), a prolific writer on the subject of borderline conditions, emphasizes pathological defense mechanisms and object relations as the core diagnostic criteria. Kernberg's criteria are a mixture of inferential judgments and direct clinical observations. In an effort to identify and differentiate stable personality constructs that develop and endure over time despite symptom fluctuations, Kernberg applies the term *borderline* to patients with the specific and stable form of pathological ego structure he calls borderline personality organization. This author postulates a total system of personality organization ordered on a hierarchy from normality through neuroses to psychoses, with the borderline patient placed between neuroses and psychoses.

Patients suffering from borderline personality organization present themselves with what superficially appear to be typical neurotic symptoms, none of which are pathognomonic. Although the presence of two, and especially of three, strongly points to the possibility of an underlying borderline personality organization, the definite diagnosis depends, says Kernberg, on characteristic ego pathology and not on descriptive symptoms.

According to Kernberg's postulates of the borderline patient, ego weakness is manifest in three specific characteristics: (1) a lack of anxiety tolerance, (2) a lack of impulse control, and (3) a lack of developed sublimatory channels for drives or desires. Kernberg also notes a shift toward primary process thinking in the borderline patient.

Certain specific defensive operations of the ego are considered the core of the borderline personality organization. Splitting, according to Kernberg, is the essential defensive operation and underlies all the others which follow. At the lower level, splitting as an active defense mechanism is said to predominate over other defenses such as primitive idealization, projective identification, denial, omnipotence, and devaluation. Splitting is the inability of the patient to integrate positive and negative introjections and identifications, resulting in a lack of synthesis of contradictory images both of the self and other objects. Objects themselves are often considered either all good or all bad.

Kernberg's speculations include the ideas that the splitting process develops around the third or fourth month, reaches a maximum over the next few months, and gradually disappears in the latter part of the first year. The entire process, then, has run its course before the development of verbalization. However, he indicates that it may be present pathologically at higher levels of ego organization, where it can adversely affect self- and ego-identity. Kernberg's postulates are impossible to test, as they are high-level speculations rather than phenomena observable in therapy. These speculations are verifiable only through direct observations of infants and mothers in natural and experimental situations.

Kernberg postulates the pathology of internalized object relations as another general criterion. As a result of splitting, an incapacity to synthesize or reconcile good and bad introjections and identifications emerges. People tend to be considered either good or bad. Sometimes, however, there may be adaptation to others. This is a pretense of acting "as if," based on the patient's ability to reenact the partial identifications which are split off from one another. The result is an ability to change markedly from situation to situation, and a consequent lack of an integrated self-concept. Masterson (1976) adds that the borderline patient recapitulates his split object relations, acquired in the developmental phase of individuation, in the treatment "transference." The borderline patient shows little capacity for realistic evaluation of others. Real guilt or feelings of concern for others is deficient; real empathy for others is unlikely. The borderline patient experiences little emotional involvement with others, and in fact appears emotionally shallow. Most wishes are angry wishes. At times withdrawal from others is a defense against intolerable wishes or feelings. Finally, underlying all of the borderline patient's relationships are feelings of inferiority and insecurity. Kernberg (1968) says that he based his inferences upon clinical findings in the transference relationship. The poor relationship capacity of borderline patients brings into doubt the validity of using the transference concept in relation to them.

Borderline States in Psychiatry, edited by Mack (1975), contains, in addition to the editor's incisive historical perspective and afterword, two types of essays: first are applications of the borderline concept as postulated by Kernberg; second are such critiques of the specificity of the concept as the explications by Guze (1975) and Klein (1975). Adler's lead article accepts the specificity of the borderline concept and considers those patients borderline who demonstrate stable character structures and the immature defenses stressed by Kernberg. In keeping with the Kernberg formulations, Adler suggests therapeutic strategies derived from an understanding of the patient's defensive organization and his presumed conflicts in the formation of object relations. Adler refers to transference and countertransference issues, assuming that early developmental defects are unresolved early life problems that can be worked through. Adler's is followed by a series of articles on therapy with borderline patients in different settings and with different groups, e.g., inpatients, outpatients, adolescents, families of adolescents, and supervised residents treating borderline patients. Another application of the Kernberg formulations—uncollected by Mack—is Groves' "Management of the Borderline Patient on a Medical or Surgical Ward, The Psychiatric Consultant's Role" (1975).

Mack himself comments, "Kernberg's postulates are difficult to test and it would be hard to find evidence that might refute some of them since they are based on intimate clinical contacts coupled with extrapolations to hypothesized infantile psychological processes, which are often preverbal and therefore not easily observable."

Dickes (1974) considers the wide variety of views held of patients termed *borderline* and takes the position that the use of the term applies the unsubstantiated speculation that health, neuroses, and psychoses exist on a continuum. Borderline states are placed between neuroses and psychoses, although according to the continuum concept borderline lies also between health and neuroses. Dickes holds that there is no borderline and that mental illnesses differ in etiology and course. Neuroses and psychoses, in his view, are not contiguous. In conclusion he regresses to Hoch's concept and suggests for the group of patients under consideration the designation *pseudoneurotic psychosis, type undetermined.*

Among those who, like Dickes, argue that the borderline is not an established diagnostic entity is Guze (1975), who specifies five steps necessary to establish a psychiatric nosological entity as valid. He contends that a verifiable syndrome requires consistent data on the natural history of the disorder and its delineation from other conditions. These criteria have not, according to Guze, been met in the case of the borderline syndrome.

Klein (1975), like Guze, holds that the specific diagnosis of a borderline syndrome has been established neither on the basis of a predictable response to psychoactive drugs (his particular field of interest) or on the basis of any other recognized criterion. Klein notes that Grinker et al. found four quite distinct groups within the borderline syndrome. These, he thinks, resemble clinically other groups of patients (not labeled borderline) who have been differentiated on the basis of their response to particular types of medication. Group II, for example—patients demonstrating certain forms of emotional instability and affective lability—resemble patients who have been found to respond well to phenothiazine drugs and to lithium. Klein also questions the diagnostic usefulness of the structural approach. His major interest is in using psychopharmacological agents for differential diagnosis, and he argues that affects lend themselves better than do these more abstract notions to the verification of the response to drugs or other forms of treatment; they are, therefore, of greater diagnostic and prognostic value.

The genetic studies of Kety, Rosenthal, and co-workers (1971) include under the rubric *schizophrenic* those individuals whose psychiatric history can be characterized as "chronic schizophrenia," "acute schizophrenic reaction," or "borderline schizophrenia" as these terms are commonly used in the United States. The concept of borderline as part of a schizophrenia spectrum ignores the views of such authors as Schmideberg, Knight, Grinker, and Kernberg, who emphasize that the borderline represents not a regression but a defect in psychological development.

Dyrud (1972) supports the concept that the borderline is part of a schizophrenia spectrum. On this basis, he considers the psychoanalytic model applicable if individual treatment is the aim: "If we set ourselves the task of treating specific ego incompetencies, is psychoanalysis the technique of choice? The answer is very likely affirmative if we think of interpretation as a way of helping the patient to develop sharper discrimination of both inner and outer stimuli, and the emotional interaction between analyst and patient as a way of shaping his behavior with direct consequences."

Pfeiffer (1974) in his article "Borderline States" claims that despite the fact that the concept of borderline states is not yet firmly established in American psychiatry, sufficient evidence has accumulated to document their existence. It is his further opinion that borderline states do in fact constitute a separate clinical entity, sufficiently distinct to set them apart from other diagnostic entities, and that borderline patients require therapeutic approaches distinctly different from those used with neurotics or psychotics. One of his guiding principles is that strictly psychoanalytic or insight-oriented psychotherapeutic approaches are by themselves never warranted.

Perry and Klerman (1977), thoroughly disenchanted with the state of the art, have become concerned for the evidence for scientific reliability and validity of the borderline concept, although they praise the research of Grinker et al. They undertook a comparative analysis of four sets of diagnostic criteria for borderline patients. The analysis was conducted as the initial phase of a project aiming to evaluate treatment of affective components among borderlines. In planning such a project the necessity of reliable valid criteria for selection and diagnosis became apparent. An exhaustive review of the literature yielded four sets of criteria for analysis: the "borderline states" of Knight, the "borderline personality organization" of Kernberg, the "borderline syndrome" of Grinker et al., and the "borderline patients" of Gunderson and Singer. These four were selected because of the quality of the clinical descriptions and their influence both on the literature and on clinical practice.

Further progress with the borderline concept, say Perry and Klerman, is unlikely without the application of scientific methods in testing our present hypotheses. Among the several possible approaches to testing suggested is the idea of collecting individual cases as prototypic of borderline patients. Such a collection would provide clinicians and researchers a reference group similar to that provided by Breuer and Freud's *Studies on Hysteria*. Another approach might involve following multiple diagnostic group studies in a prospective design through time, to find out if the syndromes differentiate themselves by a different course or outcome with or without treatment. Perry and Klerman hope, in the studies they are now undertaking, to refute or validate selected hypotheses to clear the stage for the next generation of discoveries and hypotheses about the borderline patient.

Chapter 3
Clinical Manifestations

Behavioral items observed in our research delineated disturbances of ego-functions of borderlines and were statistically analyzed into groups and factors. But to be useful to clinicians, this scientific skeleton requires the flesh and blood of recognizable symptoms.

Borderlines have difficulty achieving and maintaining affectional relations; they have trouble controlling aggressive impulses and rarely achieve a consistent, reliable, and satisfying identity. Ego-alien, short-lived confusional or paranoid-like psychoses may occur, as well as depression of the anaclitic clinging type and temporary states of loneliness which appear as depression without guilt. Absent are evidences of cognitive disturbances, looseness of associations, and hallucinations or delusions.

In this chapter we present vignettes of borderline patients who are members of the four large groups obtained by means of clustering analysis. Our protocols contained descriptions of behaviors from a large number of observers and are suitable for the rating of items derived from an ego-functions framework. Since it is not possible to use all the transcribed data to delineate typical clinical "cases," we have chosen to fill out the clinical gap with descriptions of each of our four large groups, condensed from the protocols of several patients, other individual case reports, and a previous experimental study. *In each of the case reports the essential core aspects of the borderline are italicized; the remainder are the nonspecific peripheral symptoms.*

It should be kept in mind that statistical analyses are procedures for the study of numbers of subjects, traits, or symptoms. The identified individual patient will naturally not have all the traits or symptoms characteristic of the group. A syndrome or a subsyndrome is an idealized category, stereotype, or diagnostic entity into which a patient's symptoms or behaviors make the best fit.

In defining the overall characteristics of the borderline syndrome we found anger as the main or only affect, defect in affectionate relationships, absence of indications of self-identity, and the presence of depressive loneliness. We have in this formulation both negative and positive symptoms.

Within this gestalt the various groups represent different positions. Members of Group I fail at relationship but at the same time, in overt behavior and affect, react negatively and angrily toward other people and to their environments. Subjects in Group II are inconsistent, first moving toward others for relations which are followed by acted-out repulsion, and then moving away into isolation, where they are lonely and depressed. This back and forth movement is characteristic and corresponds with the fact that these people are both angry and depressed but at different times. Patients in Group III seem to have given up their search for identity and defend against their reactions to an empty world. They do not have the angry reactions characteristic of Group I. Instead they passively await cues from others and behave in complementarity—"as if." In no other group were the defenses observable as clearly or as consistently as in Group III. Subjects in Group IV search for lost symbiotic relations with a mother figure which they rarely achieve (except when females provide an exceptionally supportive marriage), and then reveal what may be called an anaclitic depression.

In our analyses Groups I and III showed an affinity, as did Groups II and IV. This makes clinical sense because patients in Groups I and III have given up hope of meaningful relationships while those in Groups II and IV are still searching. Patients in Group I are angry at the world and their ego integrations are endangered by this strong affect; we hypothesize that they often become temporarily psychotic as a result of the overwhelming rage which destroys their weak ego controls. Those in Group III have given up even their reactions to frustration. They are compliant and passive, relate as others wish, and successfully defend themselves against angry behavior and eruptions.

Group II includes patients who are buffeted by virtue of their own ego-dysfunctions as they attempt to relate to others, become stimulated to anger, and then withdraw and suffer loneliness. Those in Group IV, on the other hand, are characterized by abandonment of any but dependent clinging relationships; when these are not gratifying, these patients develop an anaclitic depression, weeping and feeling neglected and sorry for themselves.

When translated into clinical syndromes, the four groups elicited from the statistical analysis coincide with clinical experience. In general, Group I is closest to the psychotic border, Group IV is closest to the neurotic border, Group II represents the core process of the borderline, and Group III is the most adaptive, compliant, and lacking in identity ("as if").

The positive contributions suggest that the borderline is a specific developmental syndrome, with a considerable degree of internal consistency and stability, and is not a regression.

Group I: The Border with Psychoses

CASE 1 (Dr. Wolpert)
At the time of admission to Psychosomatic and Psychiatric Institute (P and PI) the patient was thirty-year-old mother of

two who was separated from her husband and who had been living with her parents. Her children were in the custody of her husband in California. On admission she was confused as to the reasons for admission, saying, "I don't know whether I should be here or not. My father wanted me to come." In this way she disclaimed responsibility for her treatment but would accept the facilities of the hospital, ultimately taking advantage of the hospital for room, board, and social life.

Anamnesis revealed that her difficulties had begun some four years previous. On the surface she had been doing well with her husband and the children. However, she resented his seeming lack of interest in her sexually; he had taken a job as a traveling salesman, which kept him away from her a good deal of the time. As her resentment increased she accepted a dinner invitation from friends *she knew her husband would resent.* Throughout the day of the dinner and even while there she felt an aimless dread but had no insight as to why she should feel so upset. Nothing unusual occurred, however, and she returned home, going to bed without incident. Early the next morning she was awakened by pain in her left shoulder radiating down the arm to the fingers; she also had difficulty breathing. Fearing she would die, she awakened her husband, who rushed her to an emergency room. There she was told that she just had "nerve trouble" and needed some counseling.

For the next two years the patient received intensive psychotherapy from a male psychiatrist who saw her three times a week, once a week in the later stages. At one point during her therapy she became "suicidal," and although she had made no suicide attempt she was hospitalized for three months, eventually being allowed to sign out against medical advice. Toward the end of the therapy she developed strong erotic feelings for her psychiatrist, manifested in sexual daydreams. She dressed in a seductive way for her sessions, and began an affair with a neighbor. At about this time her husband became more attentive to her. She felt things were going well and terminated the treatment although the psychiatrist felt she needed more. For four months she felt relatively well, but when her lover moved to another part of the state depression set in and she sought further psychiatric care from another male psychiatrist, who concurred with her request for electric shock treatment.

Following the second course of treatment, she told her husband of her recent affair, and the marital relationship deteriorated. He began to drink, she began to drink and use drugs, and soon they separated. From time to time she would be visited by her lover, and during such periods she would feel well, but at other times she was quite depressed. Her ability to take care of the home and children deteriorated. One year before her admission to a hospital the older of her children was hit by a car and suffered a brain concussion. Following the child's recovery she granted her husband a divorce, took a second lover, and became depressed when he asked her to marry him. Six months before admission she took an overdose of sleeping pills, planned so that her lover found her unconscious, and she was hospitalized a second time. While in the hospital the court granted custody of the children to her husband, and upon discharge the patient moved in with a girlfriend. At that time she was unable to do more than stay isolated in the house and drink.

The patient's family then persuaded her to return home, where she saw a psychiatrist once a week but remained isolated in her parents' apartment. Because of increasingly severe depression and drinking, her parents forced her psychiatrist to place her in a hospital, where she stayed a month. Almost immediately upon admission the depression dissipated and she began to function with the patient group as if she were a long-standing member. She had two affairs while in the hospital—one with an attendant and one with a nurse from another hospital. All in all, she felt more relaxed and more comfortable in the hospital than ever before. Because of her improvement she was discharged. Once home with her parents, interminable arguments and drinking began. After an argument she took some pills, slashed her wrists superficially, and was readmitted.

The patient was born and raised in Chicago. She was the older of two children, having a brother six years younger.

When asked about her early life she remembered that when she was about three or four her parents lived near her grandmother's home but *she was always left out of the communication between mother, father, and grandparents.* While her parents were always "terribly devoted to each other," she felt, *"I never belonged. Maybe that is why I felt a wall around me. I can't feel."* Although she said she was always "Mother's and Daddy's little girl who never wanted for anything because of the type of family I lived in," in the next breath she would say *she was always unsure of herself.*

In high school when she was elected secretary of the senior class she noticed that the other girls who were elected officers displayed strong emotions, including crying and exuberance, while *she herself could feel nothing. In fact she reported that she could not feel anything except when she took drugs.*

The patient is aware of how angry she sometimes becomes and how her angry outburts often jeopardize her relationships. One example of this occurred in elementary school. Her mother said to her one day that if it was forty degrees outside the next day the patient wouldn't have to wear leggings. The patient was pleased because she might not have to wear the clothes that she hated. The next morning, when her mother said that she had to wear her leggings, she became angry and decided to leave home and go to her grandmother's house. She remembered walking very slowly because she was frightened, and she kept looking back over her shoulder, hoping that someone would come after her.

"This is kind of what I do when I make suicide attempts, hoping someone will save me. Finally my father did overtake me and took me home. I was glad. I was really quite relieved. When I was in California recently I told my folks over the phone that I felt like killing myself, that they did this to me. I also called my mother to tell her that I'd kill myself, but what could she do about it? I guess I just wanted to hurt her. And I told my husband about the affair to shock and hurt him, and tell him how bad I really was. *I guess I've always done things to be cruel, to hurt other people."*

The patient dated a neighbor's son, T., for a couple of years while in high school. Finally she broke up with T. and started dating W. and D. Subsequently T. asked her out again, and instead of refusing, as her girlfriends had encouraged her to do, she went out with him immediately. For a period of several years she dated T., W., and D. simultaneously. *She had no particular preference except for the boy she was with at the moment.*

Comment: This patient represents a prototype of Group I of the borderline. According to her own statement, she has never felt that she "belonged" and says very clearly that she cannot feel. Her early role assignment was that of an object of her mother's narcissism; her mother's concerns were with appearance and behavior, not with feelings. Having no help with her feelings, they were taken as signs of her badness and *she developed a self-image of worthlessness.* When she attempted independence and self-reliance, she was inhibited by her mother's controls.

Now she shows she is unsure of herself; *her self-image is that of an inferior person who must anxiously attempt to meet the standards of others. She has difficulty in feeling anything except when she is comfortable in the hospital, where there are relatively well-defined goals, or when she is under the influence of alcohol or drugs. In order to get a feeling of belonging and identity, the patient must attach herself to someone, developing an almost parasitic relationship.* Information regarding her high school boyfriends indicated that she had no preference except for *"the boy I was with at the moment."* Her elopement was an impulsive desire to hang on to someone. Because of her impaired ability to experience feelings, inward attachments can be of significance to her only when they take *the form of violent feelings, hurting either herself or others.* Thus, her relations with others are quite intense but very unstable. She is like a tabetic who has to stamp the ground to feel.

In a vain attempt to resolve her loneliness and need for attention, the patient gradually acquired the role of the sick person, her conversion symptoms, alcoholism, drug abuse, and hospitalization being the signs of this newly developed role.

Thus we see a patient *unable to form stable affectionate relationships*, to control aggressive feelings, or to develop a coherent self-identity, vainly trying to escape from depression by promiscuity, drugs, alcohol, and hospitalization.

Treatment in the hospital lasted eight months, during which time the patient's depression gradually lifted and she became more animated, even flirtatious in a little-girl manner. When frustrated in her wishes somatic complaints would come to the fore, but repeated medical consultation yielded no organic pathology. Although she seemed to be doing better, *discharge planning was difficult* and only with great persuasion did she agree to look for an apartment. Once discharged, the patient found employment. Her original therapist left the clinic within a month of the discharge, but not before the patient had taken an overdose of sleeping pills and had been briefly hospitalized elsewhere, once psychiatrically and once medically.

Her second clinic therapist saw her for some eleven chaotic months, and ten years later remembered the patient as "*a woman I never really could get hold of in treatment. I was a new therapist and she kept me running. It was one thing or another—hospitalization here or there, promiscuity, drugs, broken appointments. We never had a treatment going in any way.*"

In his descriptions of the patient at the time of the events, the therapist noted:

> She has much free-floating anxiety, along with actual anxiety attacks which necessitate therapy in various emergency rooms. The precipitants for these are not clear at present. She has made consistent demands for Placidyl so that she can take it during the daytime. She experiences some euphoric affect from it, and has used a number of doctors in the Chicago area to supply her with it. At no time in the past six months has she been able to stop taking some sort of medicine (mostly Placidyl) for longer than a few weeks. She "recognizes" the addictive potential of barbiturates and refuses to take them consistently. She has a prominent sleep disturbance, with difficulty getting to sleep. As the evening hours approach, she becomes more active until at

bedtime she's doing all the things she should have done during the day. She drinks heavily in binge-type episodes. She is promiscuous with a *prominent disturbance of object relations. She enters into hostile-dependent relationships with people and teases them with "promises" but rarely "produces."* This has been especially evident in her setting up of appointments with me, then calling at the last minute to say she is too sick, physically, to come to the appointment, seeking my help but refusing it when offered. She has phobias about riding on buses or going places. These have not been clarified. She occasionally attempts to structure her life by obsessive-compulsive activity. Characterologically, she has many hysterical features including impulsivity, shallow affect with rapid mood shifts, inappropriate erotization of nonerotic relationships, seductive behavior, naivete and *great need for "love."*

She had a *transient psychotic episode* with delusions, hallucinations, strong feelings of depersonalization, and multiple somatic symptoms elong with a conviction she was dying of a generalized "sclerosis." The precipitant may have been her perception that I was withdrawing interest in her antics. With much difficulty she could be convinced of my care for her and she would reintegrate.

On other occasions she would lie in bed and be literally taken care of by someone else. Recently she underwent a profound regression, ceased working, increased her drug consumption. The precipitant for this episode was a *conflict over dependent needs* which were only partly met by her boyfriend. She became more *scattered and angry at his refusal of her sexual advances.* After three pill ingestions (none producing unconsciousness) in three weeks, I committed her to Chicago State Hospital but she was released in four days as "not belonging there." I recently set firm limits for her around my being of use to her. I refused to see her unless she (1) stopped taking drugs other than those I prescribed for her; (2) got a job and; (3) limited her calls to me to emergency situations.

While the therapist stated that his goal was to "try to help her for the better" he felt her prognosis to be "very guarded."

I feel that this patient is in need of help and has established some kind of a relationship with me. I feel therefore that she should be continued in clinic care. My supervisor is very skeptical of therapeutic effort directed toward her, and at one point stated that he felt she was *for all practical purposes untreatable.* I feel that because I have seen her during better times in her life, and that she is capable of more mature functioning, I will continue to see her for a while yet.

The attempted continuation of treatment failed as the patient made and broke appointments, ending her relationship with the clinic one year and nine months after her hospitalization began. Our efforts to trace the patient further led only to an indirect reference to her by a friend, some four years after hospitalization. At that time she was still living in the apartment she had rented upon discharge and had returned to the job she had quit during *the course of her angry outburst at her therapist.* No further details of her life at that time are known.

CASE 2

A thirty-two-year-old female entered the hospital, *expressing anger* at the entire world. She was so outspoken that negative reactions were evoked in everyone. Nevertheless she had to have things her own way—right or wrong. At times she was so loud that she had to be controlled from inappropriate gales of laughter. When her husband called and left a message that her *sick daughter was feeling better, she evidenced no response and acted as if she had not heard.* Her appearance was that of a disheveled person who did not care about her surroundings, nor was she insulted when criticized. The patient was well aware of the schedules for various activities, yet always shuffled in late. She monopolized group meetings with loud talk. She broke the rules concerned with proper dress and frequented the male section, which was off limits. *When intensely angry she seemed to get farther and farther away from reality. There were no evidences of positive relations to anyone.*

SUMMARY

Patients in Group I do not in general achieve a sense of consistent identity and have great difficulty in establishing positive relations with others. They have apparently given up actively trying to develop object relations and withdraw more or less from the scene. *Yet they are lonely, depressed, and enraged at the environment and at other human beings.* This rage has many behavioral outlets, but these are not sufficient to protect the *ego from transient and mild dissolution of the function of reality adaptation.* Hence the transient psychoses superimposed on inappropriate, nonadaptive, and negative behaviors.

Group II: The Core
Borderline Syndrome

CASE 3 (Dr. Kayton)

This twenty-two-year-old female was a school dropout and occasional drug user who tended toward alcoholism. Promiscuous, she had had one illegitimate pregnancy and abortion. Her psychotherapeutic sessions were filled with accounts of vacillation between "Joe" and "Larry," always breaking up with one or the other. *No evidence of any affectionate relationship was ever found, not even to a dog she brought and then permitted to die,* and there were *no transference manifestations in the therapy.* "Well, I was mad all weekend. *I just seemed to have so much hate.* I don't know what the hate was about but it was there. I seem to hate everybody. I certainly hate Joe and Larry and yet, I need them too." I asked what she needed them for. She said, *"Well, I don't want to be alone. I'm just disgusted with the whole thing.* I don't really want to go back and yet I find that I am. It's like watching, waiting to see what I'm going to do next. It's almost like a play and *I have a certain role and I look to see what's going to happen in the next act."* She said, "I'm so disgusted, *I just feel that nobody cares."* "It seems that I would like to have closeness and concern and yet, when it's within my grasp,

there's something about it that seems to make me flee from it."
"Well, when you get into a relationship like that you get
trapped. At first it's fine. But then you start getting in a
pattern. You have to do what the other one wants you to do."
"It's like when I sleep with a boy for a few months. At first it's
exciting and fun. And then after a while, I just have to keep
going. Not 'cause I want to any more. Then I want to be free. I
want to get out of the relationship, and I don't know how to do
it. So then I have to start creating little incidents so that the
other one will have to break up with me. I want my freedom
then, but then, when I have my freedom, I just feel lonely
again." "The ideal relationship to me would be a two-month
relationship. That way there'd be no commitment. At the end
of the two months I could just break it off. The relationship
would just evaporate and I'd be fine. But the only criterion for
this would have to be someone else around so that I wouldn't
get lonely."

Comment: In capsule form this sector of a therapeutic
session reveals all the characteristics of Group II: vacillating
involvement with others, overt or acted-out expressions of
anger, varying degrees of lonely depressiveness, and failure in
achieving her own identity.

The patient received outpatient therapy for two years, but
her pattern of desire for and fear of closeness persisted. She
was not committed to change and developed no emotional
insight. By her own choice she stopped seeing the therapist.

CASE 4

A twenty-two-year-old bachelor clerk complained of many problems, one of which was the suddenness with which
his feelings of well-being would disappear. For example, when
his girlfriend seemed to accept him and told him she wanted
him to take care of her, all the world appeared good; when she
was impatient with him, all the world was bad. However, he
was very unsure of his own feelings toward her. At times he
felt he loved her and needed her, at other times not. When she
told him she loved him, he would have no feeling or response

whatsoever. However, when he returned to his room, he would develop a strong longing for her which would disappear when he was in her presence. *This patient revealed difficulty in achieving and maintaining affectionate relationships.*

SUMMARY

Patients in Group II still actively search for companionship and affection from others. They are involved but in a vacillating fashion. They move toward an object but soon become anxious and angry, and retreat only to become lonely and depressed. The resultant confused picture is often labeled "ambivalent," but in reality there is little real affection, only anger and loneliness. They do not become psychotic, although the to-and-fro movements in relationships to objects are confusing to the observer.

Group III: The Adaptive, Affectless, Defended—"As If"

CASE 5 (Nurse Therapist)

I got in touch with him about two or three weeks ago about coming to patient activity meeting. He was sitting at the desk in his room reading. He was very pleasant, but didn't say much. He said that he couldn't consider coming down and that he wasn't ready to do anything yet. There was really no affect at all, including no sign of annoyance. At the end of the week I contacted him about getting started with some activity and about the activity meeting. He said that he wasn't able to tolerate this group, there were too many people. I mentioned several programs, such as morning recreation, occupational therapy, and men's recreation. He was aware of these things going on. I asked him about the morning recreation program and he found cheer in the fact that he could come and observe; still, he wouldn't participate. I invited him in to sit on the sidelines in the gym; he refused. He watched the entire period, leaving a short time ahead of the group. I also talked to him about coming to O.T., and he let me know that he had been assigned to work with the group and knew what it was. He said that he didn't know yet if he would be able to attend, but promised me he would try; he did not appear. I asked him about any particular interests he had had before coming into the hospital. He said that he had particularly enjoyed bowling. He knew that we did go bowling, but he wasn't ready to do this. He didn't look directly at me, but he did turn somewhat toward me. This he doesn't always do. I had the feeling that the information he volunteered, which was more than I had really expected, was an effort to get things over with, so that he wouldn't have to tolerate the contact any longer than necessary. He didn't look really depressed; he was more withdrawn. There was no real affect. I have gone to his room to talk with his roommate, Mr. S.; they were both there, but there didn't seem to be any communication. He does leave the ward quite a bit, but he's always by himself. He seems to plan his trips to the canteen when it isn't crowded, because he is always alone. He seems to have some expectation that this is just a period that he has to go through and at some point it will be over and he'll feel better, and that's it.

He will come out and watch one TV program; then he will go back to his room and read. Then he might come out and watch another program. Then he'll go back again. He was having a pretty hard time making an adjustment to having a room-mate. Whenever his roommate was in the room, he was out. When the roommate was out, he was in. Now he is able to sit with his roommate there. How much they talk I don't know, but at least he is in there with him. Once he told me he was sleeping during the day because his roommate snored at night and he couldn't sleep. Most of the time he reads in his room.

His father visited him Saturday evening. They went to the canteen. His father came in and went straight to his room. I was in the dayroom. When they were ready to go to the canteen, his father was with him and the patient asked: "Is it all right if we go to the canteen?" I told him sure. I have never seen his expression change. It's like someone who just doesn't care about anything. He has this sort of vagueness. It's always the same. I have never seen him smile. He and Mr. S. had a date to play pool. Mr. S. went to his room and reminded him. He told him, "When I get ready, I'll let you know." Mr. S. was under the impression that he was going to be ready that evening. The pitch of his voice never changes. He just says what he has to say and that's it.

Comment: This patient is a quite withdrawn person who attempts to maintain isolation from other human beings. *He conforms very well to ordinary routines and seems to have a desire to please.* He eats well, he shaves himself every day, and he dresses appropriately; but he avoids people. His isolated attitude becomes somewhat grotesque in that even without sufficient light or with the book upside down he will pretend to read in order to avoid conversing with others. With some of the personnel his conversation is superficially jocular but without any real feeling. There's a certain teasing element in the relationship. He has a hunched-over posture as if he's trying to crawl into a shell. He doesn't smile or laugh or become angry, and his eyes remain downcast. His conversation is about sports and he does follow the sports page in the newspaper and knows a great deal about the details of baseball events.

Apparently, large groups of people, conversation within the group, and noise create confusion in him. He had gradually been able to assert himself to the extent that he admitted his dislike for the hospital food and began to eat downstairs in the canteen. He now has preferences in television programs. *He is shy and doesn't make friends easily.* Overt violence and aggressiveness apparently disturb him a great deal.

This is a patient whose relationships and outward behavior toward people are quite bland; he appears neither anxious nor depressed, nor does he overtly express anger or annoyance. *He simply isolates himself, has a kind of bland communication, but mostly withdraws from contact with people. One could ascribe hardly any affect to him.* There are no apparent hallucinations or delusions, and one can only consider him as having a defect in his total affective system in that *he is unable to relate himself meaningfully to any human being except his father.*

SUMMARY

Patients in Group III are isolated and withdrawn without even negative affect or behavior. They await cues from others and attempt to relate by assuming complementary roles. In this maneuver they constitute "as if" characters who behave as expected and often appear involved. Yet their role vacillations depend on the person to whom they adapt in a facile manner. This is how they live in a world in which they feel no personal identity.

Group IV:
The Border with the Neuroses

In our stress laboratory we have studied a group of ten adult male patients who were hospitalized on a state hospital ward for chronic cases. They were erroneously considered to be suffering from chronic depressions (Oken et al. 1960).

The depression which constituted the major symptomatic complaint of these subjects had a characteristic quality. Little deep sadness was evident. In place of a sense of heartfelt sorrow and misery of the sort which stirs an empathic response, these men communicated *a dull dejection and bland loneliness and hopelessness; they seemed defeated, discouraged, and cowed, apathetically accepting their state.* There was little *in the way of spontaneous self-remonstrance or abnegation.* However, they were free in blaming their manifest failures on lack of "breaks," maltreatment, and misfortune; they "never had a chance." Their own part in their difficulties was minimized, rationalized away, or blandly glossed over in a very facile manner. Only when pressed in this particular area did they show any sign of tension or anxiety, losing some of their composed resignation and becoming irritable and whining. Here, too, their response took the form of evasion and denial. *They took no firm stand in their own defense; mobilized aggression was weak and diffuse.* Shifts of mood occurred readily in response to changes around them. They were quite responsive to a display of interest or concern. But this, too, was devoid of force or enthusiasm. *The general picture was one of resignation, lack of involvement, and marked passivity.*

The anamnestic data were very much in keeping with these findings. All these men gave evidence of long-standing, markedly limited adjustment, frequently traceable to early childhood. The typical pattern was of a moderately stable adjustment with restricted function in a relatively protected environment, usually involving a relationship with an older woman. The relationship then broke up (or the situation somehow changed), leading to the necessity for a new adjustment. Of the six men who had married, only one was still living with his wife, and he gave a history of a previous divorce. In six of the group the precipitating factor was clearly the loss of the key relationship. Rarely was this break initiated by the man himself. When it was, it followed upon his becoming unable finally to bear remarkably intense and long-standing abuse and exploitation. Whatever the precipitant, the new adjustment called for could never be made. A passive deterioration of function ensued. Jobs became less frequent and less skilled, finances deteriorated. Alcohol was used as a periodic balm but there were few true binges. Overt homosexual activity sporadically occurred in several, but without enthusiasm or the development of any continuing relationship. Often this was used only as a device for obtaining money.

During the latter period some symptoms appeared, chiefly in the form of depression with suicidal thoughts (but seldom attempts), feelings of *hopelessness and confusion.* Any frustration called for a response of avoidance, denial, withdrawal, and flight, or when these were impossible, passive-aggressive acceptance. Solace was obtained by mutual sympathy from those similarly afflicted. Daydream fantasy was frequently used. This was of a simple wish-fulfillment type, in which they saw themselves with their troubles at an end without any intermediate steps or efforts on their part. Exacerbations, associated with periods of diminished gratification, led to deepened depression, irritability, more or less developed ideas of reference, and also some anxiety, which was at times represented as fear of going crazy or "something terrible happening to me." During such periods hospitalization was readily sought and usually resulted in rapid improvement. But there was no great urge for discharge; they had "found a home." When release was arranged they "dragged their feet" but then accepted it passively, adding it to their list of injustices.

For the most part, this group of ten borderline, defeated, and disconsolate males are unresponsive, unchangeable, and almost impervious to external influence. Therapeutic interventions to alter their mode of adaptation, whether psychological or somatic, prove of little or no avail. The more overt symptomatology may abate, often with the dependent gratification inherent in hospitalization alone. Otherwise they remain unchanged, are reluctant to return to the community on whose fringes they exist, and readily seek rehospitalization during the frequent episodes when overt symptoms recur. They represent one common type of fixed and intractable psychopathology. Yet our data indicate that they are by no means unresponsive to stress. Rather, in some ways they prove quite reactive, but their stress responses, which help in exposing the *borderline core* in many patients, both psychological and somatic, have a special characteristic. These are, moreover, quite clearly related to the patterning of their general mode of adaptation, which is so "chronic" and resistant to change.

Focus on their hopelessness also had varying effects, depending upon further implication. As long as they could keep it anchored to the present, they used the feeling to bolster their defense. But when it was connected by the interviewer to the future, and seen in terms of never achieving a wished-for state of protection and gratification, it became a threat. Thus, indications that resumption or replacement of lost relationships would indeed never occur were frightening, despite the calm associated with their spontaneous utterances of despair.

Subjects related to the interviewer with marked submissiveness and compliance consonant with their life pattern. Initial interpretation met with easy agreement. There was anxiety-motivated conciliation and placatory appeasement, plaintive appeals, or flat stubborn denial without examination of the issues.

SUMMARY

Group IV patients are frequently misdiagnosed as depressives because they attach themselves to others and react with whining, crying sadness when their dependent needs are not satisfied. Thus they overtly reveal more seemingly positive affect than any other borderline patients. *Yet they still lack a consistent identity and have no capacity to give to others. Their clinging is not object-focused but satisfaction-oriented because they have little capacity to love.*

The patients presented in this chapter, observed and described in different settings, clearly belong within the borderline syndrome as derived from our investigations. More than that, these vignettes demonstrate the fact that intergroup differences are clear enough to allow the clinician to diagnose the subcategories of the borderline. The sharpness of these differences permits a specific diagnosis from history and anamnesis without the necessity of long periods of observation or depth interviews. The recognition of a patient's membership in a particular group of the borderline spectrum may in the future have a practical value even if it is not now apparent. At any rate, the classification opens a vast area for research into possible biological, psychological, and sociological correlations.

Fourteen New Borderline Cases

For the last six years several members of the staff of our Institute (Grinker, Holzman, Harrow, Walsh, Apter and assistants) have been engaged in a clinical longitudinal study of the schizophrenias. We did not select for our sample known or diagnosed schizophrenics. Instead we accepted into the program all newly admitted patients between the ages of seventeen and twenty-eight, provided the patients and their physicians gave informed consent. We have processed approximately three hundred of these patients, including sixty-five of lower socioeconomic status from the Illinois State Psychiatric Institute, by taped interviews, ratings, psychological tests, family studies, and follow-up communications and interviews. The topics discussed in the interview were:

Age, sex and race, marital status
Outpatient or hospitalization (duration)
Family
Onset
Quality of affection
Megalomania
Use of Drugs
Depression—suicidal
Anhedonia
Anxiety
Psychotic behavior
Intelligence quotient
Thought disorder
Organization
Confusion
Flooding of stimuli
Identity
Paranoia and projections
Dependency
Sexual behavior and preference
Humor
Attitude toward body
Interview vs. behavior
Defenses
Courses in hospital
Plans for future

Of those processed, fourteen were identified as borderline. Following is their collective profile.

Marital:	10 single, 2 married, 2 divorced
Age:	18-28 years
Family:	10 mental problems of various types
Language:	No problems
Anxiety:	4 diffuse anxiety
Anhedonia:	9 early lack of pleasure
Thinking:	3 with though disorder
Affect:	10 with varying degrees of depression and/or anger
Onset:	12 in childhood
School:	12 with problems, often dropping out or expelled
Work:	3 with difficulties in holding a job
Drugs:	7 with drug abuse
Loneliness:	8 with marked complaints yet voluntarily isolating themselves
Suicide:	10 with suicide attempts or thoughts of suicide
Identity:	11 with problems
Dependency:	10 showing emotional attachment to family or surrogates
Affection:	10 with little or none
Confusion:	9 to some degree
Paranoia:	2 to some degree
Hallucinations:	None
Delusions:	None

Two new traits appeared significantly often. One, anorexia nervosa, seemed a means of indirectly expressing anger at the family. The other, having some references to early biogenetic and psychogenetic processes, was the unusual accounting of *dreams, remembered from an early age (usually between three and five years), of violence directed either outward or inward, toward the dreamer.*

The following fourteen patients were diagnosed borderline

on the basis of the clinical hospital record and the research
interview as rated by three senior investigators.

CASE 6

This is the first P & PI admission (but the second psychiatric
hospitalization) for this twenty-four-year-old white single
Jewish female who recently completed her second year of
teaching.

"I was real indecisive about my boyfriend—what to do. He
wanted to get married. So I dropped him [end of May] and then
I began to get *violent thoughts. Thoughts, 'I hate you. I want
to kill you.'* "

The patient began to experience *homicidal ideation
stimulated by her heterosexual involvement* with a man who
suggested the possibility of marriage after several months of
dating. She entered outpatient treatment and the "hate
flashes" abated, due in part (in her opinion) to Haldol. They
returned in February of the next year, at which point she
moved from her apartment to stay with her older married
sister for a couple of weeks. The symptoms recurred and have
persisted since the middle of May. The patient describes her
current situation as being much harder than during the
previous episodes—with respect to both the symptomatic
duration and the chemotherapeutic resistance. In regard to
this patient's violent ideation, *she describes her "crazy
thoughts of killing someone" as being nondirected, floating,*
and often experienced when she is alone. Hospitalization,
which was initially avoided out of therapeutic concern for her
potential for massive regression, became necessary in
response to her increasing homicidal agitation as well as to
indications of depersonalization and derealization.

The patient had been briefly hospitalized four years prior to
the present P&PI admission, in response to similar symptomatology concurrent with both an intense heterosexual
relationship and her mother's hysterectomy. Sustaining
outpatient treatment did not ensue.

The patient is the second of three siblings, having an older
married sister (age twenty-nine) and a younger brother (age

twenty); she lives at home with their mother. The father died about three years ago. In reference to family characterizations, the patient states, "My mother is very domineering. She always did everything for me. She's very good-looking, a better figure than I have.... She did what she could.... She's real good at giving you food and clothes. But she never played with me." In striking contrast she states, "My dad was fun. He used to play with me ... oh, jokes, and when I would come home from a party he would ask for all the details. My mother never wanted to know.... He was just a real good guy." The patient depicts her younger brother as "becoming like the father of the house" subsequent to their father's death. She further states that "he takes care of my mother so she doesn't go crazy." He is described in vacillating terms by the patient—as "very stubborn, egotistical, bad-tempered, [as well as] honest, sincere, trustworthy." The patient states in reference to her sister, "She's very strong, determined, dynamite sense of humor, very practical, unpretentious.... I love her very much, probably more than anyone else in the world."

The patient describes three early memories. Of the first (from about age four) she states, "I remember rocking my brother to sleep. He was an infant and real sick ... bad diarrhea, very bad. They were thinking he might die.... I think my mother was around." She immediately relates the second memory. "I remember dressing up as twins with my brother and going to Riverview Park ... like sailor suits and same shoes. He was about four, I was about eight." Her third memory was of "moving into my house—this little girl saw me step on her property (next door) and she punched me. I was five, she was four.... Her mother saw and made her apologize.... We later became friends."

In reference to recurrent childhood dreams, the patient relates, *"I was sitting at the dining room table, ready to eat and there would be a big picture of a werewolf sitting behind me. He would strangle me, always me, no one else."* She additionally states, "I used to have flying dreams. I loved to fly, it was exciting. Once I was conscious and jumped downstairs all the way from the top. . . . I hurt my knees, got bruised . . . well, it was a little one—six stairs."

Concerning her elementary school years the patient initially states "that is a total block, a blank area." She does go on to describe a current continuing affinity for art which dates back to that period. The patient also states, *"I was always scared of school—of teachers, afraid of not making good grades, of authority figures. . . . I remember being teacher's pet—a quiet kid who never caused any trouble, then freaks out later; a good freak-out never hurt anyone as long as it goes away. . . .* I was always smart—the top of the class, but very shy. People wouldn't know—*I act aggressive but inside I'm very shy."*

The patient's depiction of her high school years are *devoid of any description of friendships or activities* but rather focus on the teasing she endured subsequent to her breaking up with an eighth grade boyfriend and the sad reluctance of another boy to become involved with her in the face of the peer pressure the former wielded.

The patient attended university. Of this experience she states, "I liked the classes but not commuting." (She lived at home throughout her undergraduate years.) "College was okay, nothing special." The patient relates that her choice of university was based on the fact that her girlfriend was going there, emphasizing, "No other reasons . . . it was a poor reason; *we were hardly friends through college."*

Of her current teaching involvement the patient states, "It's up and down. The disciplining I can't stand. It's very hard, the screaming. I've gotten laryngitis. The kids don't want to learn. They expect fun and games all the time. I've started to bluff lesson plans, the kids don't know the difference."

In response to questions pertaining to her sexual history—masturbation, childhood sexual play, fantasies, age and circumstances surrounding first intercourse—she responds, "I think that's a personal thing and I'm not answering. . . . To tell you the truth, I don't think this is anybody else's business." With respect to first menses, this occurred for the patient at age eleven and a half. She describes her reaction as being "horrible, just horrible. Nobody was home. I started screaming. . . . I knew but it still scared me. . . . I had eaten grilled cheese and thought that was the problem. . . . I finally found my mother at the grocery store." She currently continues to experience very bad menstrual cramping.

The patient is unable to speak about her decision to terminate her recent relationship except to characterize the man as "a tease, sort of a loud mouth."

The patient is oriented; memory appears intact, reality testing adequate. There is no evidence of delusions or visual/auditory hallucinations. Judgment appears concrete and capacity for abstract thinking is similarly impaired by both perseverative self-reference and low frustration tolerance. Concentration is poor. There is a pervasive degree of hypochondriasis present which at times seems suggestive of fleeting emotional blocking. She is not actively suicidal and the potential for overt manifestations of the present homicidal ideation appears questionable.

Comment: This patient presents a clinical profile of borderline fragmentation precipitated by perceived demands for adult heterosexual intimacy. It may be speculated that the violent ideation stirred in her is reflective of a specious disavowal of heterosexual object relationships. Of relevance here are her facile idealization of her deceased father; her current idyllic dependence, in the absence of earlier interactive significance, upon her sister as a structuring force in her ego; her ambivalent yet interactively detached characterization of her brother concomitant with her first cited early memory; her labile response to first menses; and her guardedly hostile, yet clinging interaction with the female interviewer. It may be postulated that the *murderous impulses* described by her are stimulated beyond her agitation tolerance by heterosexual intimacy demands, but fundamentally are attendant upon a more primitive feminine identification emergent throughout the process of separation/individuation. It does appear that this patient experiences a *great deal more rage toward mother* than is expressed

(childhood crying and sulking)—albeit with hostile cynicism.
Diagnosis: Borderline Syndrome, Group I.

CASE 7

This white female patient entered the hospital at age
eighteen with the complaint: "I can't stop eating." She was
attractively groomed and dressed, but reluctant to talk with
the resident. *Although most of her life was described as
chaotic*, she became aware of emotional problems about a year
before admission, when she would become ravenously hungry
and "eat herself sick." She would then diet and, following
that, again overeat. She had no control over her impulses. As a
result she weighed eighty-five pounds when she was taken out
of college.

The patient, born in Chicago, is the oldest of three siblings.
Her two younger brothers (aged sixteen and thirteen) live at
home with their mother and stepfather. Her natural parents
were divorced when she was nine. She recalls many argumen-
tative scenes and sees the divorce as a mutual agreement for
separation. However, *she has a lot of hostility toward her
natural father*, calling him a "weirdo." She feels that her
father hates her because he hates her mother. The father, age
forty-five, is a lawyer and lives in Iowa. She sees him
infrequently. The mother is described as "caring, sensitive,
she does everything for me. I don't know what I would do
without her." The mother remarried when the patient was age
twelve. At first the patient felt angry and jealous toward her
stepfather. Later she accepted him as a likable, easygoing
man, but she still prefers her mother. The stepfather brought
three of his own children by his previous wife into the family,
and she has had ambivalent relationships with them.
Sometimes they *"fight viciously"* and other times they are
"companions." One stepsister is a year older and attends
college. This girl has also had psychiatric care at this hospital.
The other two live at home.

The patient *had as a child a recurrent dream in which people
were attempting to kill her.* She would wake up in a fright but

make herself go back to sleep. She does not remember how long these dreams continued. She was reluctant to talk about her childhood, saying sarcastically that she was a "normal kid." She was a good student in high school, but this apparently was a chaotic time during which she was "thrown out" of her home several times by her stepfather because she was *"acting like a bitch."* On one of these occasions she went to live with her biological father for several weeks. She did not date or have any sexual experience until her last year in college. She denies the use of street drugs, except occasional marijuana.

She is oriented, but her memory is blocked by emotionally laden material. Her judgment is good. There is no evidence of psychotic thought process, no suicidal ideation. Her affect is hostile, bored, but with no perceptual distortions.

Comment: This patient indicated evidences of a severe personality disorder but no evidence of psychotic thinking. There were no indications of positive relations with other humans. Her usual behavior was to "act like a bitch." Her dreams reflect anger projected toward others, who were seen as trying to kill her. We can speculate that the alternating cycles of starving and overeating represented the acting out of her angry affect, which only partially protected her against hostile behavior.

Diagnosis: Borderline Syndrome, Group I.

CASE 8

This twenty-four-year-old white bachelor entered the hospital for the second time with the complaint that he felt as if he were about to explode. He was previously admitted because of panic attacks, and he was still shaky on discharge.

The patient was doing well at his job until about six weeks previous, at which time he began to experience generalized anxiety, loss of sleep, and vague symptomatic complaints—"something was just wrong inside of me." He expressed feelings of *inadequacy in interpersonal relationships* but

could not be specific about a precipitating event except to deny
that his discomfort was related to his work. Following an
acute anxiety attack, accompanied by feelings of depersonalization, he was hospitalized for several days until his
anxiety subsided. He then returned to Chicago to see his
former therapist, who felt hospitalization was required.

The patient was born and raised in the Midwest, the middle
child of three siblings. His sister, age twenty-eight, is married
and lives nearby. His brother, age nineteen, now lives at home
but is planning to attend college in the fall. The patient always
felt close to his brother but described his sister as being cool,
aloof, and critical. His parents separated when he was sixteen
and were divorced two years later. He describes his natural
mother as "neurotic and highstrung." She was the dis-
ciplinarian in the family. Her fluctuating mood-swings were
confusing to him as a child. His mother initiated the divorce,
deciding one day to leave the family and accusing her
husband of an affair with another woman. She is a teacher.
She has never received psychiatric care. The father is
described as a quiet, mild-mannered person. He remarried one
year after divorcing his wife. The stepmother works as a
secretary for her husband. The patient claims that he likes his
stepmother and was not opposed to the second marriage.

His earliest childhood memory is of attending nursery
school at age four. He remembers this *because he was very
frightened of having to leave home to be with "strange"
children.* However, he recalls happy times playing with
neighborhood children. He attended a coed grammar school
and again describes how *fearful he was of going to school. He
felt isolated and lonely. The first three years he says he was
very depressed, overweight, and had virtually no activity
outside of scholastic work at school.* This was during the time
of his parents' separation. He would come home from school
and sit in his room or talk with the housekeeper. Finally, in his
senior year, the patient out of sheer willpower lost thirty
pounds, and forced himself to join in activities. He became the
senior class vice-president, took parts in school plays, and was

elected to National Honor Society. He dated a girl steadily until they were geographically separated by attending different colleges. He says he missed his girlfriend terribly, living from one phone call to the next, but at the same time maintains that *he really didn't feel love and that he was "play-acting." College years were very lonely. He had no friends and buried himself in studies.* He majored in science. Following graduation, the patient obtained his job and despite personal problems has done well. *He experienced his first anxiety attack and hospitalization one year after graduation from college.*

On his second admission the patient, although of large build, was not overweight. He appeared older than his twenty-four years: Dressed neatly in tailored shirt, slacks, and loafers, his hair clean and well-groomed, he *seemed somewhat hostile and impatient at the intrusion of questions.* However, he apologized once or twice, stating that he was in a bad mood and felt frustrated that two years of psychotherapy had not relieved him of his anxiety.

The patient is oriented, his memory good, his judgment intact. He is intelligent. *Affect was anxious and depressed.* He has occasionally had suicidal ideation but has not seriously considered this step. There is no evidence of psychotic thought. He has experienced some depersonalization and perceptual distortion of a visual nature at the height of his anxiety. There are no auditory hallucinations. *His emotional discomfort (severe anxiety) seems to stem from his dissatisfaction in object relations. He has marked sensitivity to loss and separation. There is also a noticeable lack of feeling toward family members.*

In the patient's first questionnaire, two years after his first admission, he states that *he has had no friends and has been very lonely since his early fear of starting school; yet he prefers to be alone. He occasionally has angry outbursts, suspiciousness and confusion.* He believes that in his unreal world people think critically of him and that his panic attacks might result in his "falling apart." *He can't make a friend and feels split into several selves.* Although he is heterosexual, thoughts of homosexuality scare him, as do commitments to girls; *he is afraid to love anyone.* Despite these handicaps, he graduated from college and has held a responsible job. Yet his childhood anhedonia, crying, and anxiety persist.

Diagnosis: Borderline Syndrome, Group I.

CASE 9

This white, married, twenty-five-year-old Catholic female entered the hospital with the complaint of uncontrollable crying, sexual problems, and a suicide attempt.

The patient married in 1967 at age seventeen. She met her husband at work, was attracted to him because of his good looks and because he seemed strong. After five months of courtship they ran away to be married. The night before, they had attempted intercourse but the patient had become frightened and pushed him away. His response was tolerant and they were finally successful in having intercourse. However, the patient said it was painful for her, *she did not want her husband to see her body and ever since then she has not wanted to be touched by him and has never experienced orgasm with him.* She said she "freezes up."

Three months after their return to Chicago, the patient became pregnant. She says she was happy about having a child but was afraid of being unable to do the right things to care for it. She had no difficulty during pregnancy or delivery. During her pregnancy, she and her husband moved into the basement apartment of his parents' home because they couldn't afford their own place. After the baby, a girl, was born, the patient and her mother-in-law began to disagree over the care of the child. The mother-in-law would criticize the patient's method of care, and since the patient was unsure of her actions she assumed she must be wrong. Within a year they moved to their own apartment so the patient could get away from arguing with her mother-in-law. After two years they returned for a while, then left again because of *fights between the patient and her in-laws.* She says her husband did not really take her side but allowed the fights to continue. In 1971 the patient again became pregnant. This was a planned child and she had no problems with pregnancy or delivery of the child, a second girl. Her in-laws had built a separate apartment in the basement of their new home.

About this time the *patient became aware of not caring for her husband*. She saw him as criticizing her treatment of the children and as never being around to support her. *Their sexual relationship became worse with less frequent contact* and she avoided his touch. She felt that she had married him to get out of her own home. She went to a psychologist for a few sessions and he told her that her sexual problems were related to her father's attempts to seduce her as a child.

About six months before admission the patient had gone back to work. Her husband and her in-laws were against this and told her that she should be at home with her children. She feels that she needed to get out of the house. Since she began work her relationship with her mother-in-law has further deteriorated. In fact, the family threatened her with violence during fights and called her a bum. She felt they were treating her like a child.

One day before admission the patient took 5 mgs of Valium. She thought the pills would kill her but she changed her mind and called a boyfriend and a psychiatrist. The latter recommended hospitalization.

Eight years ago, just before she met her husband, the patient scratched her wrists with a razor blade. She was home alone and at the last moment decided not to kill herself, put a bandaid on the cut, and mentioned it to no one. *She felt she liked nothing about herself, her personality, her behavior, her body.* She still feels the same way. This episode occurred shortly after her father had tried to run her over with her car while she was leaving his tavern and had threatened to kill her with a gun for not bringing him a soft drink.

The patient was born in Chicago. Her mother had four children by a previous marriage, three boys and a girl. The patient has never been close to any of them, was nine when she last saw the girl, and has never seen one of the boys. She has two real siblings, a sister twenty-seven and a brother twenty-two. She says her sister had polio at age three and lived with an aunt for long periods. She remembers that she resented her sister when she was home because it meant more housework for her while her mother lay around and drank. In the past years they have become a little closer. She has always been distant from her brother. She remembers her mother bringing men home to have sex while her father was at work. Her sister has told her that her mother would have sex with men in the front of the car with the children in the back. Her mother was not involved with their schooling and was not aware when the *patient began having academic problems and began missing a lot of classes.* She says her mother and father fought all the time and separated once when she was seventeen. Her father owned a tavern, and from the time she was six he tried to touch her and have her touch him. At first she *accepted,* but later avoided being alone with him. She was frightened but told no one until at age seventeen she told her mother. There was no response. At about fifteen, her father called her a whore and she had a fantasy of putting a doctor's statement on the wall saying she was a virgin. She did not remember if she and her father had ever had intercourse.

The patient began school at age six. She cried the first day but later adjusted well and liked school. *She had no close friends. In high school she began cutting classes and going to the bowling alley.* Her grades fell and she was asked to leave school in the middle of her sophomore year. Her parents weren't aware of her problems. *She had no close friends* and no extracurricular activities. She then went to beautician school for six months, but felt she couldn't pass the exams. Shortly thereafter she met and married her husband.

The patient began menstruating at eleven or twelve. She had not been told what to expect and was frightened. A neighbor explained menstruation to her. Her periods have been regular but with cramps. She began dating at fourteen but had no steady boyfriends. She had no voluntary sexual experience prior to marriage. When she was fifteen, her stepbrother visited home and twice tried to undress her, which she resisted. She denies masturbation, sexual fantasies, or homosexual contact. She has no reaction to her contact with either her father or her stepbrother and remembers only parts of what happened.

The patient is an attractive young woman of normal weight who looks her stated age. At her first interview she was neatly dressed in slacks and blouse and her hair was curled. She shows no unusual gait, tics, or psychomotor retardation. She speaks at a normal rate, with normal inflection, and is clearly understandable. Her relationship with her interviewer was appropriate, with hesitation at discussing intimate matters. She is an attractive person, relates well, and is oriented and alert. Her memory of events before age six is vague and many gaps are present in recall of the traumatic events in her family. Her judgment in realizing she needs hospitalization is good.

Abstraction: She did not understand proverbs. Her insight into her illness is minimal with little idea how her family relationships have affected her behavior. *Affect is appropriate, with crying when expressing feelings of loneliness,* and no abnormal shifts in mood. Her thoughts are well formed with good ability to follow an idea logically. She evinces no abnormal speech patterns, and denies auditory or visual hallucinations, distorion of her body parts, depersonalization, or paranoid ideation.

Her failure to form peer relationships and her poor school performance after puberty may have been related to her feeling unfit or undesirable—low self-esteem fostered by her guilt over sexual impulses directed to her family. Also, her poor social adjustment was accompanied by a feeling of inadequacy and shame.

Comment: Born into a disturbed family of a rejecting mother and a father who used her sexually since age six, *the*

*patient grew up lonely and violated with no close or casual
friends, failing at school and work, and suffering from low
self-esteem, considerable confusion, and a loose integration.
Anger is directed toward the rejecting family of in-laws.*
Associated with her early sexual experiences, sexual satisfaction can only be attained outside the marriage, adding to her
confusion and feeling that someone will come into her room
and hurt her. She has never enjoyed life or loved anyone,
including her children, who receive little attention from her.
Even the final solution of suicide twice resulted in failure.

Diagnosis: Borderline Syndrome, Group II.

Faced with the demands of the *WAIS* and the *Proverbs Test*
to think and perform, she blocked, stated her ignorance, and
gave up with no attempt to perform. Her tolerance for anxiety
is low, and she attempts to cope with it through withdrawal
and constriction. She was a little more comfortable on the
Rorschach where she was permitted to be introspective. Her
style remained defensive and constricted, but she was able to
produce integrated, reality-appropriate responses. She tends
to strive for greater integration and organization than she can
really pull off—anxiety, self-criticalness, possibly depression
interfere with that. She is threatened by affects, her perceptions becoming vague and less organized as she protects
herself against their potential explosiveness. Thus, there is
some suggestion of a paranoid character style.

CASE 10

This is the first P&PI admission for this twenty-nine-year-
old, single, white Jewish male who has recently terminated
his work as a hairdresser. Prior to admission he had been in
psychotherapy for ten weeks.

The patient states: "My mind was running away from me,
just like a bummer acid trip. I felt acute anxiety. It seemed like
life was at an end. I was thinking self-destructive thoughts,
having obsessive thoughts of suicide, and I was panic-
stricken. I realized I was going through a severe change in life

and I could no longer capture the thread of continuity, optimism, you feel when you're well." He also observes, "I lost my clientele, job, apartment, and identity, in that order."

For eight months in 1975, the patient was in treatment, terminating four months prior to his P&PI admission. The termination was precipitated, the patient states, by his conviction that the therapist was "not giving me enough. I felt deceived because I had regressed and felt like an infant and needed more." At the time of the termination the therapy was also dealing with issues related to the patient's father and his suicide. Ten weeks prior to his admission he began treatment with another doctor.

In January the patient turned twenty-nine, which acted as a catalyst to his sense that "I saw others achieving while I saw myself as not doing anything ... a nothing!" At this time he felt limited in his work and by December had lost his job. He admits that "he asked for it. *I lost my clientele through my indifference.*" He became progressively depressed, with loss of appetite and sexual drive, and began sleeping ten to twelve hours a day. He moved to his mother's home and found himself increasingly "panic-stricken" at his suicidal thoughts. He discontinued use of Navane "to see whether I was crazy or not" and as his anxiety mounted, he accepted his therapist's recommendation for hospitalization.

The patient's earliest memory is of a positively toned, anaclitic object relationship: "I was two years in the crib. My mother would have guests and come in to check me. She patted me and I had secure feelings. I felt secure, warm, good, happy...." It is interesting that he also claims to recall banging his head to lull himself to sleep during this period. Recurrent early dreams include (1) driving in a milk truck which sprouts wings and flies under the patient's control, and (2), dreamt between the ages of nine and eleven: *the patient is outside his house and knocks on the door; a frightening, witchlike woman's voice says "come in"; a man grabs him, crucifies him to the wall, and stabs him while the woman watches. He recalls that his primary fears in childhood*

*concerned separation from his mother and being afraid to ask
to go to the bathroom.* The patient feels that he was a "happy,
secure, well-adjusted" child during his early elementary
school years. He recalls having close companions (one boy, a
number of girls) and playing primarily girls' games.

He describes his father as a "cool, detached, aloof man" who
was also "violent," beating him with a strap to ventilate his
rage. The beatings started at nine or ten years of age. The
father reportedly was diagnosed as a paranoid schizophrenic,
who felt he was being poisoned and plotted against. The
father appears to have been actively psychotic and delusional
from the time the patient was twelve or fourteen. When the
patient was sixteen, the father was admitted to a hospital and
hanged himself the next evening. The patient remembers
feeling relieved, but notes, "I buried feelings that turned into
guilt that I didn't do anything for him because I didn't
understand . . . and for feeling relieved."

The patient describes his mother as "inept. She was
incapable of being a strong parent. I always felt more
powerful than she." He recalls that his mother would try to
interfere with, and protect him from his father's rageful abuse,
but could provide little real protection. He states that his
grandmother, who "doted" on him, was "more of a real mother
than my mother." Apparently during his early school years
the grandmother came to the home on a daily basis to take
care of him.

The patient recalls feeling embarrassed by his pubertal
changes and attributes this to his wish not to become like his
father. "He made me embarrassed of masculinity. He was a
weak father, but he made such an issue of being physical and
violent." At fourteen, the patient engaged in mutual masturbation with another male adolescent, finding it "pleasurable."
Afterwards, he reports, "I had a cold and frightened feeling—
'you're homosexual.' I felt panic and fear that I was different,
really different." He reported to his mother that he "had a
problem." She told him "it will probably go away" without
inquiring further, leaving him with the feeling of being

ignored. The patient had no further sexual contact until sixteen, when he started dating girls (with whom he "petted" but had no intercourse). He dated three girls on a regular basis and notes "I flunked high school because of one girl. It was puppy love.... We cut classes together."

When he was twenty-one, his mother remarried and pressured him to leave home: "I left a sheltered home to become a hippie in Old Town." The transition was earth-shaking. *There followed an extended period of identity diffusion. He states, "I felt terrible, lost, misplaced.... I couldn't seem to find anything." The patient describes himself as "devastated by dope ... speed, PCP, MDA, and acid five times a week."* Between twenty-one and twenty-five, the patient's work and sexual histories are chaotic. *He "job-hopped," working as a hotel clerk, in other clerking positions, and as a theater manager.* At twenty, he had had his first "meaningful" homosexual experience and began a "promiscuous" pattern of homosexual contacts, "hanging out in gay bars and turning tricks" to supplement his income. The patient states that he has *"never had a lover or stable relationship"* and feels bad about this. During this period he felt "degenerate and demoralized."

At twenty-five, he went to school and subsequently took a series of jobs, the most stable of which entailed working eleven months at Bonwit's. For this brief period he "felt secure and happy, but still promiscuous." In 1972, he went to San Francisco, "to get myself together." While there he saw a psychiatrist, but after falling into much the same pattern of promiscuity and drug abuse he returned, "demoralized," to Chicago early in 1975.

In March or April 1975, the patient saw a psychiatrist twice weekly on an outpatient basis. He terminated treatment because the "therapy had become painful" and the therapist refused to provide medication. The *patient remarked, "I felt deceived, because I had regressed and felt like an infant and needed more."* Subsequently he began psychotherapy with his present doctor and feels the therapy proceeded well because "he was strong. I needed to feel he was magical in order to believe in him." The patient also pursued a brief course of psychotherapy in California. He has had no previous psychiatric hospitalizations.

He had no unusual childhood illnesses, and his surgical history consists of plastic surgery (for the nose) in 1972. He reports minor use of alcohol, but intensive use of psychoactive drugs (MDA, PCP, dextroamphetamine, and LSD).

The patient is oriented, and his thinking, as process, is well organized with no evidence of cognitive slippage. He is clearly an intelligent young man and converses about himself fluently. His capacity for self-observation is greater than average; it appears that his previous treatment has resulted in, or enhanced, his interest in psychology. He exhibited only mildly depressed and anxious affect during the interview. He related in a comfortable and personal manner with the examiner. No delusional thinking, current or past, was apparent from the interview. He denied any experiences of auditory or visual hallucinations, except under the influence of hallucinogens. He denied any homocidal ideation, but has been distressed that he might commit suicide. His suicidal thoughts appear ego-dystonic and he has not (reportedly) considered specific suicidal measures. He disclaimed any current suicidal intent.

This patient presents a history of a young adulthood marked by severe, *protracted identity diffusion. His work life has been chaotic. His interpersonal relationships have been highly unstable; he has been unable to establish any significant enduring relationships. He complains of a persistent sense of internal emptiness, chaos, and confusion.*

The patient reports a relatively benign latency period, traumatically disrupted by the father's erupting psychopathology. The father's deterioration and assaultiveness coincided with a critical period in the development of adult identifications and identity. The father's defectiveness apparently rendered him unusable as an identification figure and catalyzed in the patient an active, defensive struggle against a male identification and the adoption of a female one as more adaptive. The patient's homosexual identity thus represents both a defense against the fear of becoming like his father and the ready availability during adolescence of alternative female identifications. He has been left with much residual confusion about who he is and what he wants to be, as well as deep-seated fear of recapitulating his father's fate.

In the absence of presumptive symptoms of an early or recent psychosis, and in view of the *patient's lack of an integrated identity, his recent chaotic and impulse-ridden lifestyle, his polymorphous perverse sexual trends, and his intact reality testing and thought processes*, his psychopathology appears to be of borderline severity. Currently he appears to be in the midst of a full-blown "crisis of identity," precipitated in part by a psychologically important birthday. He feels that the intensity of this crisis, with its attendant anxiety and depression, has been heightened by his semideliberate loss of job and apartment.

Therapist: What was the reason for your coming into the hospital? Breaking up with your partner?

Patient: There were other things as well. I felt inadequate, not just sexually, though sexually I did too. Not having anybody to love had a lot to do with it. I don't feel I have been a successful homosexual either. I don't know really what my sexual affiliation should be, because I don't get any happiness out of being homosexual either. I think that if I had somebody to really love, or who loved me, it wouldn't be so important what I did, but I didn't have anybody to love, and I didn't know what I wanted to do, and I've just been in a rut. And it just seems to have gone on for so long that I couldn't take the monotony of my life anymore and so I think I just started getting obsessed on certain thoughts like suicide and things like that.

Therapist: You withdrew into a cocoon and isolated yourself? And when you looked out of your cocoon?

Patient: I just saw nothingness. Everything seemed to be one-dimensional. Everything was black or white. I began to have a very existential feeling about life. That there was no

reason to be alive, and yet I didn't want to be dead either.
There was just no purpose ... there was no purpose to being
alive, and yet I was afraid to be dead. That's where the
anxiety came in. It was like standing on top of a precipice
and looking down. Like when you are very high up and you
feel pulled down. You feel curious and you feel repelled at the
same time. That's how I would describe the anxiety. Like
falling into a hole, into darkness.

Therapist: Do you have any optimism at all about the future?

Patient: My only hope right now is to have peace of mind and
to be successful at something, and not to question
everything so much.

Therapist: (To the interviewer's question, the patient indicates wanting to come out of his cocoon. Interviewer points
out this would take a certain amount of energy.)

Patient: I feel anger now. I feel anger at the hospital and that
I have to be in here. I feel anger with myself. But I don't
necessarily know where the anger is coming from. I think
that some of it is directed toward my mother. That seems to
be coming up in my therapy quite often. I think because I
was happy at one time, and because my mother got
remarried and I had to leave the home, the unit where I was
happy. I feel very angry at my mother right now.

Diagnosis: Borderline Syndrome, Group II.

CASE 11

"I'm self-mutilating—although now I've stopped since I was
in a hospital and have been able to talk about my problems."
This is the first P&PI admission for this twenty-year-old white
female, transferred from another hospital where she has been
hospitalized on a temporary holding basis for seven weeks
pending admission here.

She admits to her *self-destructive episodes* occurring at the
end of high school, but states that her real difficulties
stemmed from a car accident that she had the summer just
after she graduated. It was not a serious accident and
although she had a few bumps on her legs, she did not go to a
hospital and her doctors told her nothing was broken.

She went off to college and majored in physical education. *She made a poor adjustment, doing very badly in school— flunking world history and English, the latter because she didn't like the teacher.* She began to have some trouble with her leg and came home. She got a job in a bank, but the leg continued to bother her and several doctors were seen. She was hospitalized for evaluation and after a while she was seen in psychotherapy as an outpatient for a time. It got so that she was unable to continue to function in her job; she always wanted to leave early and *finally could hardly make herself go to work at all.* She has no idea what it was that caused her to feel this way. She was admitted to another hospital then in June 1975. There is some question as to when exactly it was discovered she was addicted to amphetamines. (She had begun taking them when she was about a sophomore in high school. They made her feel better and helped her forget her troubles.) She was hospitalized from June through August of 1975. There were a couple of incidents of harming herself there, for instance, burning her hand against a radiator. It also appears that she made no progress. She describes herself as blacking out and not remembering anything connected with incidents of harming herself. After discharge, she was not able to handle things at home or at work. *She kept to her room and avoided the family.* The patient claims that she was able to relate very well with several of the staff in the hospital, but nonetheless, *for what reason she is not aware, she slashed her wrist.* This was evidently quite dramatic and scared her very much, especially as she was put into the more restrictive intensive care unit. She claims that she had never wanted to kill herself but feels that this time she came close. She did a lot of thinking and decided that she was worth more than that, and from then on she would be at home with everyone and try to get better. Consequently she feels she was able to relate much better and make some gains in working through her problems.

There were apparently no problems connected with her mother's pregnancy or delivery. The patient was breast-fed. She was always a very shy baby, and remembers standing

outside the door of the classroom in kindergarten and Sunday
school. There is another vividly remembered incident in
kindergarten: she was afraid while the other children were
singing, and *she hid behind the piano and sat down and
refused to be dragged out by the teacher.* When she was very
young she had a lot of *horrible nightmares,* none of which she
can remember. *At first she would be too scared to get out of
bed, but then she would run and sleep in the bathroom, which
was between her room and her parents, keeping the light on.*
In school her work was always barely adequate and *she had
almost no friends.* She was always very good at sports though.
From sixth through eighth grade her free time was mostly
spent in cheerleading and doing gymnastics. She felt that she
was actually very close to her eighth grade teacher, just as she
had become quite attached to many of the female teachers she
had had through her school years.

When a sophomore in high school she had one close friend,
whom her parents considered a bad influence. They thought
the friend "used" their daughter. This infuriated her and
made it even more difficult for her to get along with her
parents. It was then that she began taking amphetamines.
Sometimes the two girls would cut classes together.

It was through the encouragement of a female gymnastics
teacher that she went to college, where *she very manifestly did
not do well.* She managed her physical education courses very
well but could not handle world history and biology because
they were too hard for her and English because she didn't like
the male teacher. She left school after one semester.

Her menarche was at age fourteen, and her periods were
extreme but very infrequent, sometimes as few as one or two
times a year. Her mother taught her about sex. She has never
masturbated or had sexual intercourse. In high school she had
but two dates, to the Prom in both her sophomore and junior
years.

The patient came home from school when she began having
trouble with her left leg, a painful bruise appearing suddenly
where she had sustained a similar bruise in the car accident of
December 1973. She somehow cannot now remember or care to

remember many "details, which are all a matter of my record if you'd read it."

At the bank where she worked, she had made a girlfriend with whom she had begun to get quite close. *The patient was never close in any way to her parents*, although the relationship has improved lately, because she has now told them that she will be honest with them in the future and tell them exactly how she feels about everything. At the time she was not able or willing to describe her parents any further. Her two brothers have seemingly rejected her; the twenty-one-year-old refused to come and visit in the hospital, and the twenty-four-year-old, who is not at home, called her up and told her she was very stupid, and was generally not very understanding. Her seventeen-year-old-sister she never got along with at all, and the fifteen-year-old she doesn't have much to do with. The latter always played up to the father, which upset the patient very much, especially as he never seemed to catch on.

She is of medium height, slightly obese, and very neatly, cleanly, and not unattractively dressed. She was rather nervous, with a quiver in her voice and a mild degree of hand-wringing and preoccupation with her cigarette. She arrested her gaze almost the entire time, only occasionally looking sideways or straight at me. Her posture was erect, her gait normal, her face expressionless to almost sullen. She was in fact a bit hostilely indifferent, and not overly cooperative, refusing to remember details and stating that her history was both a matter of record and irrelevant. There was, however, no hopelessness or suicidal tendency, and her replies were otherwise spontaneous, relevant, coherent, and goal-directed. There were no discontinuities in the stream of thinking or looseness of association, no flight of ideas or distractibility. Her thinking was realistic without preoccupations or delusions, hallucinations, paranoid ideations, or ideas of reference. Her orientation was intact. She was fairly attentive, and had no difficulty with recent memory or concentration. She refused to interpret proverbs, stating in almost all cases that they didn't mean anything to her or else that she had never heard any of them. Estimated intelligence is average. She did not show any insight although she stated continually that she had made great strides in understanding herself during the last month. Her judgment was appropriate in situations posed but otherwise minimal.

The patient's problems clearly began back in early infancy. The mother describes her as from the very beginning very different from the two older children, both of whom were boisterous and loud and very active boys, which was what the mother was used to. *This extreme shyness*, which she alone of the five children had, was aggravated by the fact that she was also the only one who had to struggle to achieve barely average marks in school.

Her shyness was first noted by her parents at about six months, when apparently she was very fearful. She would *cry when she encountered strangers* in the supermarket, an indication of some disturbance even at that age. At three, incidents began of *noninvolvement at Sunday school and continued through the early grades.* More important, the parents accepted this and did nothing about it. In fact, in a family in which closeness and dependency were important qualities, the patient was always seen as different from the rest, as having particular problems.

The mother was superficially engaging, affable, and outgoing, but also demanding, controlling, and obviously unable to deal with this third child, withdrawn and anything but outgoing, so different from her two boys. The mother seems peculiarly rigid and unable to adapt to this. In encounters with her mother she always gave in, keeping the peace and allowing her mother to superficially control her. She seems nonetheless to be having some difficulty handling the separation from the family, as currently she is studying abroad.

Comment: The patient, *unlike her sister, did not have the capacity to display even superficial affection for her father, or anyone else for that matter. She could display only anger and resentment,* as shown in such comments as "How could

Father be so blind as not to see how my sister acts?" She could not give in to her mother's demands, but instead resisted. This only exacerbated the entire situation. She had no friends until a sophomore in high school, and the one she made then was unacceptable to her parents. Her feeble attempts to protest this rejection of her minor success in making contact with others met with marked opposition by parents. It was then that she began taking amphetamines. They made her "feel better" and allowed her to forget her problems. Probably they made her feel alive, bringing her out of the numbness she must generally have felt. She has admitted to this numbness, which she described in the past as "blacking out" during her self-mutilation episodes. These episodes were attempts to attract the attention of her family to her plight and also to make herself feel alive. Notable here is the violence she inflicted on herself in order to reproduce the pain and bruises she had incurred in the auto accident.

When she does escape from her blandness, her affect is hostile—anger concealed in disgust. She makes a *minimal adaptation to any environment,* seeming often to comply by simply not not-complying or rebelling. *She usually forms very superficial relationships which evaporate easily or are apparently intensely felt, dependent relationships.*

Psychological Tests Administered: Wechsler Adult Intelligence Scale (WAIS); Sentence Completion Test (SCT); Draw-A-Person (DAP). Psychological tesing was requested primarily to ascertain this patient's ego strengths and her capacity to mobilize such strengths in response to unstructured test material.

The patient's behavior during the testing situation may be characterized as extremely passive-aggressive. She appeared superficially cooperative during the initial testing session, perhaps because the structured WAIS permitted her to maintain a distant stance which did not preclude a minimally adaptive responsiveness to the test items. This minimal responsiveness broke down, however, as she approached the more difficult items in each of the subtests on the WAIS. Her manner of responding to what she does not know has a shamming quality that seems indicative of an exceedingly low tolerance for frustration. Beneath a somewhat supercilious veneer, she appeared quite frightened by performance expectations and was unable to respond to any efforts made by the examiner to create a more relaxed testing environment. *Her relationship with the examiner remained superficial and distant throughout the three diagnostic contacts.* Additionally, she engaged in behavior aimed at disrupting an alliance between diagnostic efforts and therapeutic objectives—for instance, by distorting what ensued in diagnostic sessions, the patient effected a split between the therapist and the examiner.

The patient's performance on the WAIS resulted in a Verbal Test Score of 95, a Performance Score of 96, and a Full-scale I.Q. Score of 94. This places the patient within the (low) normal range of intelligence. There is a minimal degree of intertest scatter present on the WAIS which may be indicative of fluctuations in personality functioning (e.g., the high score on digit symbol). The most prominent finding of the WAIS, however, is her extremely low tolerance for frustration.

The patient's responses on the Sentence Completion Test do provide some insight into what is immediately distressing on a conscious level. These include the difficulty she feels in forming a therapeutic alliance with her therapist, a generalized distrust of the hospital environment, and *substantive fear with respect to what others think about her.*

Her two drawings indicate low self-esteem with respect to both body image and the development of a heterosexual feminine identity. It may be suggested that the superficial quality of her drawings, along with her refusal to relate in any way to what she had drawn, are illustrative of the defenses she employs when faced with issues of bodily integrity and a conflictual struggle for autonomy.

Organicity may be ruled out on the basis of available data, as may any question of an underlying chronic schizophrenic process. Probable defenses for this patient encompass both repression and denial. She appears to function more comfortably in highly structured situations but it remains uncertain how seriously immobilized by anxiety she may become when faced with unstructured tasks. The fluctuations observable both in performance and in interpersonal approach/avoidance behavior seem to indicate her substantive need for a continuing imposition of structure and consistent limits.

Diagnosis: Borderline Personality Disorder with passive-aggressive features, Group II.

CASE 12

This is a twenty-one-year-old single Jewish female who appears quite sensitive and relaxed but somewhat depressed. Throughout her conversation there is a smooth shift in affect from happy to sad issues. Her ability to reflect on her own motivation and needs shows superior intelligence.

The patient recently completed four years of college and this January plans to take a year off from her studies. In the middle of her junior year in college, when faced with depression she delved into her studies more deeply in an attempt to achieve more and more and thus stave off painful feelings of depression. *She has been depressed for as long as she can remember, and even as a child remembers coming home and not finding her mother (since her mother worked all day long) and wishing her mother was home.* As a college student she saw the clinic psychiatrist on four occasions but didn't like him. At present she feels she can benefit from psychotherapy and enjoys the idea of being in the hospital in a protective environment and away from the pressures of her family.

Her father has always worked as a tailor and her mother has always worked; the family has led a low economic existence. Her earliest memories involve visiting the hospital with her father to see her newborn brother. She connects no affect with this memory. She also relates that as a child she was embarrassed to bring childhood friends home because her parents would fight and yell at each other. They have been sleeping in separate bedrooms for as long as she can remember, and she says that they are separated at least emotionally. The patient exhibited childhood disturbance in the form of bed-wetting but denies any serious phobias, recalling only a fear of getting her clean dresses dirty since her mother was super-meticulous. The patient sits sucking on her thumb and is very anxious about the biting, the sucking, and the resultant chronic irritation. She played all kinds of games during childhood and had the average number of childhood relationships, but whished that her parents got along better. Puberty came on at fourteen and the patient reacted with shock. She describes her mother as being quite prudish at that time but "more with it now." The patient has never had sexual intercourse although she has dated boys in college. *She seems very uptight regarding sexual matters.* She says she enjoys making out with boys but never feels sexy except in the very early morning, when she first arises, but then she turns it off. *She dated boys in college but has not done so for the last year, noticing herself withdrawing more and more from her friends and social contacts, avoiding parties and other social get-togethers. She fears rejection more and more. Her greatest fear in dating at this time is the fear of being rejected by a boy if she should become involved with him.* She relates, with some smiling, a dream that she had in college of playing pool and what it meant to her symbolically. She says, "I was feeling horny then." The patient has never worked and wishes to return to college to enter law school. She says she dislikes social sciences, would not like to be a social worker or a school teacher, but has completed four years of college. *Her leisure time is spent reading and listening to music. She does not enjoy physical activities.* The patient sees her mother as overprotective. The mother is also described as the manager who keeps the house going, even while the father is characterized as a domineering person who criticizes the mother when she does not attend to his needs. When the mother became angry with the patient as a child she would react by just being silent. Now, however, the patient sees her mother as a friend. The patient has one sibling two and a half years younger with whom she has a normal brother-sister relationship.

The patient wears no makeup and is dressed in a bathrobe. Her gait is purposeful, with no psychomotor retardation. Her posture is relaxed. Her body build is difficult to determine but she is neither excessively obese nor thin. She appears to be quite feminine and is an interesting conversationalist, although she is never showy. Her general behavior level is one of incapacitating and painful depression. She exhibits no unusual motoric behavior except sucking on her thumb and index knuckle. She appears to enjoy conversing with the interviewer although she blushes at times when approaching sexual information or information involving closeness. There is no attempt to distance herself although it is plainly evident that she has some conflict about how close she wants to become.

Mental Status showed that she is oriented, her memory adequate, her judgment somewhat impaired. Her intelligence is above average. She is able to concentrate and subtract serial sevens from 100. Her abstraction ability is adequate. She showed a good observing ego although it is somewhat lacking in affective expression. *She says she is able to express anger verbally, cussing and shouting, with people she knows well. Despite being moderately depressed and incapacitated* by this lack she feels hopeful that psychotherapy will help her out of her depression and give her the support she needs to further her academic achievement. At times during the interview she smiled and there was a normal shift from one affect to another. She exhibits no thought disorder or looseness of association. Her syntax is within normal limits. She exhibits no language abnormalities. She denies any perceptual distortion such as auditory or visual hallucinations.

For her father this is the second marriage. She says that her mother was raped in her early twenties by a man she was engaged to. The mother is prudish, overprotective, and masochistic, doing everything for her children but nothing for herself. The father is described as ineffectual, throwing temper tantrums, but never able to accomplish much on his own. Because the mother worked even when the patient was a small child, one can surmise that the early mother-daughter relationship was not close. And because the patient sees herself as very self-centered, one can further surmise that the mother's self-esteem as well as the patient's was never adequately developed. *The patient does not appear to have had a lasting, meaningful relationship with a peer during her development and her ability to relate is doubtful. The patient has in the past dealt with chronic stresses through attempts at academic overachievement while avoiding more painful interpersonal relationships.* She does not appear to have established the basic trust normally developed in the first two years of life. *She has a tendency to deprecate herself as not having accomplished anything by graduating from college, and does not see herself as feminine and attractive, although she could very well be if she would wear a little makeup and the proper clothes.* Attending law school seems a masculine venture and one must suspect that to be a woman, as viewed from the patient's life circumstances, is a passive, degrading, nonsatisfying, and masochistic existence.

Diagnosis: Borderline Syndrome, Group II.

Comment: This patient complains of having been "depressed" all her life, but the *essence of this feeling is really loneliness.* As a child she recounts her reaction at not finding her mother at home after school. *She has had no lasting meaningful relations, avoiding people for fear of rejection. She cannot let herself become involved with people. As a lonely person she feels inferior and is afraid of testing herself in new situations. Her only affect is anger at the people she knows best. She cannot correctly assess other people's motives, fearing rejection, which is a projection of her own defenses.*

A two year follow-up revealed more friends and acquaintances and an informal engagement. She has had two years of law school, and lives with two roommates at school. She now says she prefers to be with others. There are periods of self-confidence, but *angry outbursts and rages* still occur. Despite these, there are some periods of fun and happiness. She says that she has been helped "slightly," which she attributes to a "general process of aging," but considers herself "still not a happy person."

The psychological tests do not suggest schizophrenic pathology. Problems of control over impulses seem noteworthy.

Full-scale IQ is 123, verbal IQ 134, and performance IQ 104.

CASE 13

This is an unmarried nineteen-year-old Jewish boy turned Catholic. In March of 1975 he attempted suicide with a drug overdose and was unconscious for four days. This was his second attempt, and was made because he saw no way out of a hopeless situation in which life had no meaning. Yet despite his existential despair he believes that the will to live has now won the battle against drugs.

The patient is the oldest of three children. His parents were divorced when he was five years old, his mother remarried when he was eight, and his father is now married, for the third time, to a black woman of thirty by whom he has a ten-week-old son.

The patient's earliest memory was of his mother accidently stepping on and squashing his pet turtle. She punished him for playing with it in the living room. When the patient was four, the carriage he was playing in was set afire by his brother. Walking alone in the woods and exploring nature was the patient's favorite boyhood activity. His brother was a "ratfink" he could not endure, nor could he stand his stepfather, who was a "sports freak."

Masturbation began at eleven and heterosexuality at twelve, at which time he began to drink excessively and smoke to excess. In addition to frequent periods of drunkenness, he began using amphetamines at age fourteen. The patient ran away from his stepfather's house to his own father, but within a year he ran back to his original home. He could endure neither. For a year he was a male prostitute in a southern city.

At one time he saw a psychiatrist for two and a half years at his mother's insistence but hated it because he received no counseling and learning about himself produced no motivation. He had no friends to discuss his problems with. Medically, he had a collapsed lung and thought he was going to die. He describes himself as physiologically and psychologically addicted to drugs.

He appeared quite bright, pleasant, and cooperative with the interviewer, and showed no signs of psychotic processes or impaired cognitive functioning. He was coherent, organized, oriented, and reflective. But he does not feel himself to be real, requiring the strong stimulation of alcohol, drugs, and sex to evoke internal sensations. He feels like an actor seeking reactions and motivations from others.

Diagnosis: Borderline, Group III.

Psychological tests: Although there is no evidence of schizophrenic thinking or reality distortion in this record, there is the suggestion of an idiosyncratic, arbitrary view of himself and others. There is a defensive hostility, a depreciation of others and of himself, with some guardedness and constraint in expression of affect. He is somewhat introspective; oral, anal, and sexual impulses tend to color his language and thinking. He has concerns about his own sexuality, his appearance, and his body integrity and intactness.

CASE 14

This is the first P&PI admission for this twenty-two-year-old, white single male, living at home with his parents. The patient was admitted on April 14, 1971 and discharged on April 16, 1971. The purpose of hospitalization was to avert an impending psychosis. Due to the short length of his hospital stay the admission summary is taken from the written record.

"I get sort of manic-depressive. I was very low last week and did a foolish thing." The patient then described a severe "low" after being rejected by a girl. He said he was "odd man out in a triangle." After that he felt life was not worth living and there was no use facing another day. He cut his left forearm with a

razor blade and said, "I didn't care if it ever stopped bleeding."
It did. The patient has always been a loner. He graduated last
June from college and has since been working.

The patient had an operation for a cartilage removal from
his left knee in 1966 following a wrestling injury. He also
suffers from hay fever.

The patient is an alert, attractive person, intelligent and
oriented. He appears coherent without obvious thought
disorder. There is perhaps some evidence of a minimal
tangential quality of speech. He appears anxious in a
controlled, subdued way. There are no obvious hallucinations
or delusions. He says he is sensitive to what people think of
him.

Research Interview Data: The patient describes a constant feeling of futility which caused him to attempt suicide.
*Socially unsuccessful in elementary school, he was ganged up
on, and laughed at.* Even his supposed best friend rejected
him. He had always to prove his own worth. In college he had
a B+ average and was on the dean's list. But work was difficult
because he could not get his mind off his problems. *Girlfriends
rejected him, for which he blames himself.* He has substituted
psychiatrists for a family. He is very anxious and cannot sleep
at night. *For four months he has lived a life of isolation so
lonely he aches inside and hates himself. He cannot elicit
positive responses from people and suspects no one can love
him.* He is perfectionistically clean and orderly and is
obsessed with working out physically to achieve what people
want from him.

Diagnosis: Borderline Syndrome, Group III.

Psychological Report: The following observations on the
patient's psychological functioning can be made on the basis
of his performance on several psychological tests administered at the time of his first follow-up visit some *three years
after his hospitalization.*

The patient is a man of superior to very superior intelligence, having an IQ of at least 120 and probably higher.
His excellent intellectual performance was marked by

occasional but brief breakdowns on easier task material. The patient appears unable to use his formidable intellect to transform painful or primitive thoughts and associations; his record shows almost no human movement responses on the Rorschach. His fantasy life is marked by a noteworthy amount of sadistic and oral imagery and by impoverished object representations. Such traits are not surprising in someone suffering from limited or painful interpersonal relations. Despite these negative findings, there were no overt signs of thought disorder on the patient's record.

Follow-up revealed that the patient is still depressed and that neurotic symptoms persist. He has a negative outlook on life, poor social functioning, no friends, and a poor work history. He has a negative evaluation of his own functioning, and exists only by working for his father.

CASE 15

The patient came to Chicago approximately one month ago to be with a man-friend. Since then she has felt that this man's daughters, twenty and seventeen years old, hate her because they are jealous. During this time the patient has suffered from insomnia and severe headaches. She was given Cafergot for the headaches, but when she took it she found she developed hallucinations. At one point she thought that she couldn't move, that there were insects crawling over her, and she hallucinated a spider on the wall. She also has experienced episodes in which *she was talking to people and did not realize they weren't there.* After a few minutes she would turn and see that they were not present in the room with her. During the episode when she thought she couldn't move, she became very frightened and called a physician who recommended hospitalization. She understood that her headaches might be exacerbated by emotional difficulties and she came to the hospital for that reason.

The patient was born out of wedlock and does not know who her father is. She feels that she is a product of a love relationship, possibly the only true love her mother ever had.

She has two older sisters, two years and four years older, who were born in wedlock. Her mother has been married five times in all. During the patient's early childhood her mother had emotional difficulties and the patient spent much time living with grandparents and aunts and uncles. These relatives were very religious; she describes them as fundamentalists. She found it easy to fit in with their way of life—*to be a good girl,* go to Sunday school, and get a white Bible for perfect attendance. Later in life she had no particular interest in religion. She felt that she was the favorite of all the people in the family. Her earliest memory is of living with her aunt and uncle, and she remembers she wanted a beautiful doll, which they bought for her, making her very happy. She felt she was always given whatever she wanted, even more so than her sisters. The patient describes her mother as very "screwed up," a person who would do things for you and be very nice but then after a while would feel that she had been taken advantage of. The patient returned to her mother when she was two or three years old, and her two sisters joined her. They had been in an orphanage before that time. Her mother was married to a man for whom the patient had no feeling, despite the fact he was nominally her father. The patient spent most of her early life traveling throughout the Southwest with her family, as her mother would frequently change homes and names. It was at the age of eight or nine that she was told by one of her sisters that she was illegitimate.

The patient started first grade at age five, because she was too bright for kindergarten. She did well in school and liked school until the fifth grade, when she felt that *things were going too slow for her and she became bored and began to skip school.* At the same time she became *attached to a teacher,* the only important man that she can remember in her early life. He understood her difficulties in school and he and his wife wanted to adopt her. He was her fifth grade teacher. He arranged for her to advance in school and she skipped two grades so that she finally graduated from high school at fifteen. The patient tells me that her IQ is 165. At age ten she began dating a boy across the street. He would carry her books and they would kiss and hold hands, but there was nothing more between them. She says she never masturbated and even now does not do so. At thirteen, the patient tells me, she had her first affair. She says she looked very sophisticated for her age, and at that time looked older that she does now. She thinks the man thought she was eighteen, and says her mother also treated her as a very sophisticated person and liked to confide in her; therefore, the mother did not mind when she became involved with this man. She continued a sexual relationship with him until the age of fifteen. Until her recent relationship, however, she feels that her *sexual relationships were very unsatisfying*. She began working at ten and has always liked to work. At that time she worked as a waitress in order to get the things she wanted. She bought enough clothes then to wear a different dress every day for a month or two.

After graduating from high school at fifteen, the patient left home. She did not go on to college because she felt she could make more money working. She went to San Francisco and worked as a cocktail waitress. During that time her headaches began and she *felt depressed*. She again had a close relationship with a man, this one lasting four years. At sixteen, she made a *suicide attempt*, taking some pills and cutting a wrist, and was admitted to a hospital overnight. She was not kept there the next day because, she thinks, the man she was dating had a lot of influence. When the headaches began, she described them as "hanging over her head like a death penalty." At seventeen, she became pregnant and went to Mexico for an abortion. She tells me this does not really bother her now. When she was nineteen and working in a San Francisco nightclub, she met her future husband, who was singing in the club at the time. He developed pneumonia, and she took care of him; he became attached to her and they married having known each other only a few weeks. She describes him as a man with great charisma, but very introverted at times and often alone, and depressed. The patient felt that their marriage was happy for five years, and they have two daughters, now two and a half and four and a half. When her husband became depressed because his work was not going well, they separated, decided to try it again, and then separated once more. The patient wanted her marriage to go well because her mother had had so many divorces. However, she found that she acted more as her husband wanted her to than as she really felt like acting. One of the arguments which contributed to the separation was that she wanted to work as a cocktail waitress, and her husband did not want her to work at all. She likes to work as a cocktail waitress, she tells me, because of her *fear of loneliness, especially at night.* Often she even sleeps with someone simply to fend off that feeling of loneliness. She remembers *wanting to sleep with her mother as a very small child.* Her later relationships were always with men and she has never had a close woman friend. After her marriage to her husband ended, she stayed by herself for a period without any close relationship. Then she called up her present boyfriend on a pretext. She had been attracted to him when she met him but nothing had come of it while she was still married. He is the first man with whom she has had an orgasm. She describes him as very considerate, not like the other men she has known, who all felt that sex was mainly for them. He takes time with her and she feels he really cares whether she responds to him. The patient has had psychiatric treatment once in the past four years—a month of hypnotherapy—followed by visits to a psychiatrist who treated her with pain medication, Mellaril, and Valium. She feels the only relief she has ever gotten from her headaches was when she was given Demerol and Thorazine by a psychiatrist in a hospital emergency room.

The patient is a neat, attractive girl who appears slightly anxious but still likable. She talks almost nonstop and seems to feel it essential to tell me how important all the people are that she has dealings with, and how special she is. She is extremely willing to answer any questions I might ask, and never appears hesitant, though she did skirt the issue of her divorce three or four times, getting off the subject before answering my question about why she had wanted a divorce. She is clearly very intelligent. Orientation and memory are intact. Cognition is normal and thinking is not concrete. Around the time of the examination, the patient was having occasional hallucinations of the type she described—talking to someone, then looking around to see they were not there— but these were almost certainly due to her use of Cafergot for approximately six days. There was no evidence of any suicidal intent, and the physical examination was within normal limits.

Comment: This divorced woman with two children has played an "as if" role all her life in an effort to please others. As a child she was passive but *unstable and continually fearful, as demonstrated by her nightmares.* Nevertheless she has had a good work record and was an A student, earning scholarships. *Yet she fears criticism and therefore strives to please.* She *feels uncomfortable in asserting herself and when angry*, she feels like an empty shell and split into parts.
Diagnosis: Borderline Syndrome, Group III.

CASE 16
The patient, for whom this is a first psychiatric hospitaliza- tion, is a nineteen-year-old, single Jewish male. "I came into the hospital because I can't go on living so uncomfortably. Last year I was functioning well. *I need the hospital to be cared for, and not a job, where the attention wouldn't be on me.* I was making life miserable for my parents. I was taking attention away from my sisters. I would talk constantly about my problems. I would scream at night and in the morning, 'Please God, help me,' in my bedroom. I would shake in the bed and gag in the morning. *In the evening I would go into a room and scream and later pant like a baby."*
The patient was attending university for the academic year 1973-1974. It was his first year of college. He states, "well, actually I left the university in March. I couldn't study any more. Things broke down. I was cheating on tests. I flunked language. I came home on spring vacation and saw a psychiatrist. He said I wasn't ready for college, but my parents sent me back. *I lasted a day.* I was going to see a

hypnotist to get through the semester, but I saw a psychiatrist instead and he gave me a medical leave of absence. I came home and got a job with a city bureau. My dad got me the job. I wanted to fail but I did the job for two weeks. Then my dad got me another job where I'd worked last summer. I had done a great job last summer but now I was not doing so well—I was obsessed with myself. I stayed eight weeks but felt that I couldn't live this way."

On Mother's Day the patient felt a compelling need to harm himself. He went into a cedar closet and took seven of the twenty Dalmane tablets in his possession. He came out of the closet and informed his parents, who then called his physician. The latter "interpreted this move as a sign of either fighting, growing up, or staying as a baby."

One day the patient went to a hardware store to buy poison to kill himself. He informed his mother of his intentions and spent some time trying to decide between weed killer or ant killer. He did not buy any and came home to find his mother in tears. The patient relates that *he began to cry because his mother was crying, but he does not know how he really felt.* He states that *"over the years my anger has built up,"* and that he is presently ambivalent about his life and his future.

The patient is the eldest of three siblings in an intact family. He describes his father as, "a quiet person. I don't find that he laughs that often. He's serious. I feel very close to him. When I was at college, he called me three times a week." The patient now calls his father three times a day for reassurance. He says, "He was understanding and always said to come to him when I had problems. 'I'm here for you.' He's not bossy but I find that he has a strong influence on me and makes many suggestions."

The patient states, "Mother would take care of me when I was a child. She'd take me to the park. I loved her and we'd have a good relationship. She was understanding. She said, 'come to me.' When I was being taunted by other boys, she said to fight like a man." He feels that he has been compared unfavorably to his cousin all his life. His parents also have worried about money all of his life. The father is less successful than his brother and is compared unfavorably. The parents fight frequently. The father is strict with money and calls his wife "a spoiled woman." The patient believes that his parents love each other but are not real close. He has always hated one sister and fought bitterly with her. He feels closer to another sister who is more like him. She suffers from a cleft lip and is shy.

"I remember going to the park with Mother and watching trains go by" (age three or four). "I remember a nursery school where I was yelled at. I was yelled at in general. In the first grade, I was bringing chairs to the reading group and hurrying. The teacher yelled and I cried" (age five or six). He does not recall recurrent childhood dreams or nightmares. *He feared his parents would abandon him when they went out for an evening.*

The patient reports that he was obsessed with religion in the sixth and seventh grades and would talk only about Hebrew school and how well he did there. He read the Torah for the cantor.

He wet his bed sporadically until age eleven and still bites his nails. He reports setting fires with another boy at age eight or nine. He always "played with matches." As a child he had temper tantrums and violent outbursts.

He reports that as a young child he made few friends and that between the ages of six and eight he was seen by a psychiatrist once a week. Psychological testing was done at that time.

He did have a few friends until the sixth or seventh grade. He once went away to camp for eight weeks. *He would, however, talk to only one boy there, whom he had known at home. He believes he started withdrawing at the age of eleven or twelve. "I just knew. I felt that I wasn't a part of the group and I had no friends."*

The patient has masturbated from the age of fifteen. His fantasies are of boys taking showers. He also thinks of girls and "once saw an X-rated film and thought I might like to try that." At the age of eleven, he performed fellatio on a friend. This continued for about one year, about once a week. Once he was in his bedroom with his friend when his father, suspicious, banged on the door; the patient was terrified. For four months he refused to tell his father what had occurred but finally confessed. He had subsequent homosexual experiences at ages twelve and seventeen. On the latter occasion, the partner performed fellatio on him. He enjoyed it but felt guilty, so he informed his father, who told him, "I don't want you to use your penis until you're married."

He had impulses to kill his uncle's entire family. He reports a desire to kill his grandmother as well and states, "I have always wanted to kill my sister Leslie." He denies visual illusions or hallucinations, as well as any auditory, gustatory, tactile, or olfactory disturbances. He states that he has always felt people were talking about him behind his back. He denies feelings of being influenced from the outside or of fusing with others, but states that he experiences minor drifts in and out of reality into fantasy. He has experienced panic before speaking in public and when he dropped language courses at college.

He fantasizes himself in a coffin, with his father and mother crying. There is a large crowd in attendance and everyone is saying what a nice person he was. During high school he would picture himself dead with no one at his funeral.

Once he had an impulse to cut himself with the electric knife. His desire was to cut his back and his wrist, and he actually started to cut his hand. (This was before Mother's Day.) He recalled his grandfather cutting himself accidentally with a knife and the rush of red blood which ensued. He mulls things over endlessly, feels indecisive, and can't get problems out of his mind. He has a feeling that he was destined for a great future and that he was meant to go East and become successful in international business.

The patient is a neatly dressed young man who looks about fourteen. His voice is high, his manner excessively polite, and he presents himself in a timorous, ingratiating fashion. *His posture varies from one of helplessness, openly seeking reassurances as to his mental health and ability,* to a grandiose stance of omnipotence. Due to his many psychiatric encounters he appears to be insightful in his self-observation, but *there is an "as if" quality to his behavior.* His mannerisms appear slightly feminine. One senses that his intellectual reach exceeds his grasp, and his verbalizations have an unreal quality. He attempts to mirror the examiner in the encounter.

Comment: Despite his attention-getting gestures toward suicide, the patient is not really depressed. This and other indications are part of a *strong need for constant dependent gratification.* He was moody and shy as a child; no other children came to his house. *He is a partially structured person relying on obsessive patterns. Both working and studying end up with confused states,* and he has had to strain to receive satisfactory grades. *Crying and sulking, inactivity and projected blame on others are characteristic. Anger breaks through in the form of fantasies of killing, and hostility have dominated his life, thereby increasing his defenses of dependency.* Follow-up after a year indicated practically no change.

Diagnosis: Borderline Syndrome, Group III.

CASE 17
This twenty-five-year-old single Jewish woman entered the hospital because of drug abuse.

The patient states that she had been taking Fiorinal in increasing amounts since the age of fourteen, when they were prescribed for her "migraine" headaches. However, the current psychiatric episode began approximately ten months previous to her hospitalization. At that time she experienced an increase in her emotional difficulties and a concomitant increase in the amount of Fiorinal she ingested. She was working then as a ward clerk in a hospital and staying with a male cousin (who had suggested that she move out of her parents' house in Chicago to stay with him and his wife). The patient viewed her *dependent life as relatively satisfactory at this point: she felt comfortable staying at her cousin's house,* did not mind work, and was feeling fairly relaxed and at ease with herself in forming relationships with new people.

One year ago, her cousin and his wife moved. The patient did not anticipate that this would cause any great hardship, but within a few days she became involved in a relationship with a man and moved into his apartment. She describes her immersion in this relationship as having a *driven quality to it*, and is *able to comprehend neither her attraction for him* nor her reasons for entering the relationship. A few weeks later, the patient became physically ill. At the time, she did not know what was wrong, although in the winter of that year, she had been told that she had had pneumonia and possibly infectious mononucleosis. Her new boyfriend seemed resentful of her illness and need of attention, so he left her. After a brief stay in his apartment, and then at that of a friend of her mother's, she was set up in her own apartment by her father, who had flown out to see her. His response to her continuing emotional distress was to give her a fancy apartment with a dishwasher in a building with a swimming pool.

In a few weeks, *the patient's ability to function had diminished.* She would spend many days in bed, unable to shop or cook. Her attendance at work became sporadic, her appetite diminished, and she lost weight. Use of Fiorinal increased to approximately twenty-five pills a day, and for the first time the patient had to resort to illegal means (forging prescriptions at work) to assure herself of an adequate supply. She felt "lousy" about having to lie and steal to get the drug. *She also felt "out of it," unable to do anything, and old feelings of "no self-esteem," and "I can't deal with people" became very prominent.* It was during this period also that the patient experienced her first seizure: sudden loss of consciousness preceded by a brief spell of nausea, and followed by a period of confusion lasting several minutes. These occurred once or twice a day at first, but their frequency had greatly increased by the end of the year. On several occasions she was injured or burned as a consequence of her falling.

Her parents insisted she return home. When she complied, she was immediately hospitalized. During this relatively brief hospitalization, she was not given Fiorinal, but she felt so miserable that she could not tell how lack of the drug might be affecting her. Following her release, she stayed with her

parents and continued taking a large number of pills. One
evening in early March, she attended a party with an old
acquaintance. She drank a great deal of alcohol, *felt very "out
of it,"* and had her friend drive her home. Concerned that she
might have endangered herself, the patient told this female
friend of her drug abuse. Her friend replied that the patient
indeed had a quite serious problem. Upon arriving home, the
patient passed out and was revived by one of her sisters. She
told her parents about the history of her use of Fiorinal, and
several days later they agreed that she should be admitted to
P&PI to be withdrawn from the drug.

Fiorinal had been prescribed for her for the first time when
she was fourteen years old as treatment for migraine
headaches, from which she suffered from the age of six. These
headaches consisted of auras of visual patterns, followed by a
generalized headache during which she could not tolerate
noise or light. She remembers having them frequently during
her childhood, although by fourteen their frequency had
decreased to once or twice a year. As a child she had been seen
by many neurologists, who had expressed conflicting
opinions concerning the headaches, the normality or abnor-
mality of her EEG, and the appropriate treatment. By the time
Fiorinal was prescribed, the migraines were no longer a major
problem for the patient. However, she found the pills effective
in preventing the *"tension headaches"* she had begun to
experience. Most significant, however, was the "high" that
the patient would experience when taking the prescribed dose.
Her usual feeling about herself at this time, and for several
years previous to this, *was of being "shy and stupid": she felt
herself to be mediocre as both a student and a person,
awkward in her relationships with other people, and lonely.*
The "high" made her feel more comfortable about herself, as
well as better able to face other people.

Despite the drug, *the patient remained largely isolated from
other people. She would go to high school, where she had no
close relationships, and then at home would spend time in her
room watching TV, listening to her stereo, and reading.* As she
continued in high school, she gradually made the acquain-

tance of a circle of people who constituted the "hip" group, that is, students who were using drugs (principally marijuana) and who were interested in radical politics. Her contact with them was limited to these activities. To her previously described routine were added sitting by herself in her room smoking marijuana and participating in peace demonstrations. By the end of high school, the patient's use of Fiorinal had increased to approximately six pills a day, the amount required to give her the high. She did not view use of the drug as a problem, and it was as much part of her daily routine as brushing her teeth.

The patient enrolled at a university for the summer semester immediately following high school. She states that the moment her parents' car pulled away from her dormitory, *she felt alone and inadequate. She made no friends, and spent the next three weeks in her room smoking marijuana.* In addition, she had her one acid (LSD) trip at this time, and described the feeling induced by that drug as "paranoid" and "shitty." Finally, she called her parents to say that she wanted to come home. She felt miserable at the thought that *she had not "made it" away from home and away from her parents.* A plan evolved for her to accompany some cousins who were planning a trip to Europe. She agreed to this, but soon discovered that she and her cousins did not get along. She regarded them as "unhip," that is, not interested in drugs or politics, and after many quarrels, she left them and continued to travel by herself. She had no itinerary, and at first was rather apprehensive about how she would manage. She describes first traveling to Sweden from Italy, and on her arrival in Sweden meeting a girl at the train station who was friendly, and with whom she took a train back south to Germany. Not being forced to flee back home at once gave her a liberated feeling. Despite this, on her return home she *lived with her parents for the following two years.* Eventually she attended night courses (principally in psychology) at a local community college, and took her job as a ward clerk. She remained friendly with some of her high school acquaintances who were still in her suburb, but had *no close relationship with anyone at this time.* The patient continued to use Fiorinal.

Shortly before her twentieth birthday, one of the patient's friends from high school was hospitalized for a drug overdose. While visiting him she felt that the potential for an emotionally close relationship existed, and they started to date and have intercourse. Shortly thereafter, the patient and her boyfriend moved into an apartment together. She suspects that her parents had strong negative feelings about her involvement with this boy, but tended, as usual, to blandly accept the situation rather than admit they thought something was wrong. She describes her boyfriend as very dependent, emotionally demanding, and intensely jealous of her contacts with anyone else. She was a maternal figure to him. After approximately two years with him, she describes herself as feeling an acute sense of betrayal when she discovered he was mainlining heroin. She states that, in a way, she must have known all along that he was using it, but that she ignored it until the evidence became overwhelming. The patient moved back home, but her feeling that part of her wanted the relationship to continue was strengthened by the boyfriend's own insistence that the relationship go on. They met clandestinely, because she felt embarrassed about letting her parents know she was still involved despite her loud protestations of how betrayed she felt.

The patient has had a number of psychiatric contacts, the first at age sixteen. She has seen seven or eight outpatient therapists, none for more than a year. *None of them made much impact on her, and she is unable to give any sense of what the process was like.* To none of them did she mention her use of Fiorinal, since she did not regard it as a problem.

The patient is the oldest of three siblings, all females. Her father is described as a successful businessman who is logical, intelligent, and pragmatic. The patient feels that he looked to her as the family member who might be his companion in intellectual discussions, and his successor as a radical (both parents were involved in radical politics). She remembers long discussions with her father, going back to at least third grade, and her sense of excitement and superiority to other children whose concerns were more trivial and political beliefs more conventional. The patient sees her own radicalism as a heritage from her father.

The patient's mother is described as a very dependent person whose primary concern is for things to "look right," involving a preoccupation both with keeping the house immaculate and with maintaining a happy appearance— even if this meant blandly denying unpleasant situations or feelings. One particular aspect the patient remembers from her childhood is her mother's intolerance of any rivalry between the children. This upset her mother very much; she viewed it as an extremely serious problem. Otherwise, the mother had a great stake in appearing tolerant and progressive, for example in sexual matters.

The patient describes herself as quite rivalrous and contemptuous toward her elder sister, and simply distant and contemptuous toward her younger sister. Both struck the patient as quite conventional, and she connects this with the feeling that her father had singled her out as his heir. There is no history of psychiatric contact for any other family member.

The patient describes herself as doing fairly well and having friends in the early part of grammar school. However, beginning in the later years of grammar school, *she was a loner, feeling shy and stupid, having no friends, and being a mediocre student.* She was told throughout school that she was an underachiever; the only subject in high school in which she did better than C was history, a subject she identifies with her father's interests. She earned a few college credits at a community college. principally in psychology.

Her menarche was at age thirteen, and she remembers feeling good about it; she knew what was happening because of sex education provided by her school and by her mother. Her first sexual intercourse was at age fifteen, but she says that it was not a very meaningful experience. Her only emotionally satisfying sexual experiences were with the boyfriend with whom she lived. She states that she cannot remember any fantasies during intercourse. She also cannot recall when she first masturbated.

The patient looked her stated age, was dressed appropriately, and was able to give a coherent narrative of her difficulties.
There was no evidence during the interview, nor any
behavioral indication, of the presence of a thought disorder.
Homicidal and suicidal ideation were denied.

She presents herself as someone chronically depressed, who
feels, in her own words,*"shy and stupid," unable to perform
such age-appropriate tasks as forming and maintaining
school relationships.* The extent of her feeling of emotional
depletion is indicated by the fact that despite the *abuse of a
drug whose effect is to make her feel better* about herself, and
better able to face people, she has been unable to satisfy her
own expectations of reasonable functioning. These failures
include *inability to live independently of her parents or
parental substitutes, inability to work and care for herself,
and inability to have emotionally satisfying relationships.*
She tries to use drugs and relationships to overcome her
feeling of depletion, but these maladaptive methods of
soothing herself and raising her self-esteem (drugs and
relationships whose appeal is the fantasy of being taken care
of) only confirm a *sense of helplessness,* and in any case are
inadequate to maintain her self-esteem. That she emotionally
equates drugs and relationships is indicated by the fact that
as soon as her cousins left California she was driven to become
involved with a man. Both relationships were attempts at self-
soothing, and her inability to give any description of what the
man was like indicates the *impersonal nature of the function*
she attempted to make him serve.

The picture of her mother as at once demanding and
dependent, but with a stake in maintaining a facade of
normalcy, leads to the speculation that the mother could not
make herself emotionally available to the patient in certain
crucial ways; in particular, the mother's intolerance of rivalry
between the children suggests that she may have had
conflicts about her ability to give to the children, as well as a
problem in dealing with expression of hostility. Both may
have ill served the patient's attempts in infancy to achieve
separation-individuation. The tie between the patient and her

father, centering on their radical-intellectual interests, represents most likely not a fantasy of a secret incestuous relationship excluding the mother, but rather a turning to the father in hope of an emotional response her mother could not provide. For someone whose maternal environment was more favorable, or whose father's interests conveyed more genuine emotional tone, these interests might have served as a focal point around which a greater structuralization of personality might have been achieved. However, this second chance was inadequate to the patient's needs.

Diagnosis: Borderline Syndrome, Group IV.

Comment: When this patient was first interviewed by us in 1976, we could not differentiate between so-called tension headaches and migraine, nor exclude the possibility that the patient suffered from the frequent migraine-epilepsy combination. It was also possible that the convulsions were associated with the large drug dosages. *What we can state is the absence of thought disorders and the presence of poor self-esteem, loneliness, great despondency, and poor affectionate and social relationships from early life. She could not deal with people.* The core problem is neither schizophrenia nor migraine-epilepsy, but a borderline syndrome. The deficits occasioned by this painful syndrome pushed the patient into the use of drugs to make up for her empty, lonely feeling and low self-esteem. This drug substitution, one of the possible secondary phenomena of the borderline patient, unfortunately not only failed, but worsened her general condition. Her lack of real affection was associated with a *driven* quality in her sexual relations.

CASE 18

The patient reports that she has been unable to sleep, which has prevented her from functioning well as a social worker. She feels that during the past several months she has been unable to get in touch with the reasons for her depression and constantly fears that she is going to fail socially and professionally—this in contrast to her usual competence. The

depression started in February or March, just when she had
graduated from college and was looking for a job. She was not
aware at the time that this was the precipitating factor but
now sees that it was. *She felt incapable of doing the therapy
that she'd been trained to do for two years. She states she
could not tolerate the anxiety of not understanding her clients
or not having them get better. She wanted to control this
situation.*

Sleep disturbance continued through February and March
until May. She tried the Mental Health Service at her
university, and they referred her to a private therapist on the
assumption that, since she had a job lined up for July, she
could borrow the money. The therapist, an analyst, did not
want to prescribe medication. She then went to a psychologist
and returned to the analyst in panic. Her last session with this
man dealt with her own self-destructiveness. She woke up the
next morning thinking about this and of the *possible failure*
that lay ahead. *She decided that if she was in fact going to fail
she might as well get out now.* She took fifty-five Deprol,
eleven Elavil, and fifteen Dalmane, which she had left over
from the student health service prescription. She had talked to
a friend the night before and mentioned her suicidal thoughts.
The friend kept phoning all day and finally got two other
friends to go to her apartment at seven P.M. There they found
her lying on the floor of the bathroom. She was taken
immediately to the hospital, where she spent several days on a
medical unit. She was then transferred to the psychiatric unit,
where she got what she considered inappropriate treatment,
treatment geared more to psychotic patients. The dean of her
school intervened and had her transferred to our hospital.

The patient currently suffers from serious physical com-
plications from a fall incurred at the time of her overdose. She
damaged the perineal nerve in her right leg. She is in a great
deal of pain, pain which will unfortunately continue until her
nerve begins to grow back properly. There is some possibility
that if it does not, surgery will be required.

There are no other previous episodes of mental dysfunc-
tioning for the patient, although she did note that she has had

sleep disturbances at various times since college. While she was married she took sleeping pills but had no episodes like this one. She notes she has always been hyperactive and feels this may have *masked a depression which has been building up since the breakup of her marriage in 1973*, and which in turn might be traced to the death of her father when she was eleven.

The patient was born and raised in the South. Her father was retired and she was the only child. She lived a very *secluded life* and went to nursery school at two and a half. Her mother was thirty and her father fifty-eight when she was born. She remarked several times that she had had an unusual family situation in that her father was retired and so was always around the house. But at his death all the money was lost and his wife and daughter were left in considerable financial need. After the very affluent life they had lived while he was alive, the mother had to take a job as a secretary, and they lived a much more modest existence.

The only early dream she remembers is of falling, though she would always wake up before impact. She then remembers dreams of dark water where she couldn't see anything. She also had dreams of trying to walk and run but being unable to move. The patient reports normal childhood milestones but notes that she was very hyperactive and that her teachers always had trouble with her. *She daydreamed to the point where she wouldn't even hear her name when called on.* Eventually the teachers were concerned enough to recommend the mother send her to a doctor to be sure her hearing was all right. In high school she was unable to urinate regularly, and she connects this and her sleep disturbance with difficulty in letting go. She also says that as a child *she often talked to herself in her head* as if reading a book, but adds appropriately that this isn't unusual for a child who spends a lot of time by herself.

Her favorite games were playing with dolls, dressing them up, and reading books. She also remembers playing in the woods with friends, building forts and things like that. She says she had latency-age friends. She'd gone to a small private school and there was a group of them who were quite close.

She remembers beginning to masturbate in high school, reporting no specific fantasies other than occasionally of boys she was going with. She has had no homosexual experiences other than one exploration with some girls her own age during latency. She says she has occasional fantasies of homosexual activities but it is more an intellectual understanding and never involves anyone she knows. Her first intercourse was at fifteen in the tenth grade, and that was after one year with a boyfriend she went with for two years. During the second year they had sex approximately once a week, usually on the weekend. *This began a pattern that she has not broken to date: getting out of one relationship and going directly into another.* She traces a series of men since this first boyfriend, noting that after him she went successively with one man for a year, two others for six months each, and then one for two years or so. Finally she met her husband, whom she first went with and subsequently married. After her marriage she began another relationship, which ended in March of this year. *She says she has always needed a guy to validate her self-esteem and for security reasons.* She told this last man that she was depressed and was only using him but he did not leave her until March, when they finally separated.

The patient says she has always had girlfriends from adolescence on. She says that they were pretty close, though not as close as some people. She is still in touch with one such friend. She would not talk about her family with these girlfriends, but about sex and things like that. Currently she has two very close and supportive friends, one a man and one a woman. She describes her friend as "a really terrific person." One gets the sense of real object relatedness as the patient describes her friends.

She described her marriage as beginning to slide when her husband entered graduate school in the second year of their marriage. He became progressively more involved with his friends and this drove them apart. They grew distant and the communication between them broke down. Finally he had an affair, and though she thought separation appropriate he begged her not to leave. She warned him then that if there was another affair she would have to end the marriage. They moved to Chicago and shortly thereafter the husband had a second affair. The patient left him. She states that she is sure the only reason she was able to leave her husband was the fact that *she was enrolled in school and that this gave her some structure to leave to.*

The patient has a rich job history. She first worked in New York City as a caseworker for the welfare department. While her husband was in college in Boston she worked for three years as a social service supervisor in daycare and Headstart, supervising paraprofessional people who in turn coordinated medical, dental, and mental health services for the children involved. She also worked her most recent summer as a counselor in a camp for mothers from the city.

She reports no religious history except that when she was in junior high and early high school her mother made her to go to church and Sunday school.

Academically she was mediocre to average until the tenth grade, when she caught fire and got good grades. She has made A's and B's ever since. As a college undergraduate she always made the dean's list. She had a brief experience in advertising after graduation but left to join her boyfriend in Boston. She has just earned a graduate degree in social work.

She reports no leisure-time activities, mostly for lack of time. She adds that when she was married she got into crafts and enjoyed that very much.

She says that her mother has told her of several miscarriages, but the patient has no memory of them and in fact thinks they may have been before her birth. She was told also that when she was approximately five years old her parents were told by the father's doctor that they must abstain from intercourse because of the severity of the father's heart condition. When asked to describe her father, she says that she doesn't remember very much about him. She does remember that he was funny, that he played and joked with her a lot. She was eleven when he died and has little memory of him or of her mourning him. She said her mother got very preoccupied with financial matters shortly thereafter. She reports that at that time she and her mother began sleeping in the same room. There she would hear her mother sobbing late at night, when she thought her daughter was asleep. This upset the patient very much. She shared the room with her mother for a few months, perhaps as much as a year. She describes her mother as extremely independent emotionally, and for years not close to anyone. Her mother in fact considers people "a pain," although superficially she's very warm and easygoing. The patient had difficulty in *describing her relationship to her mother, saying only that she just didn't know.* "She was concerned about me and very strict. She's also affectionate in her own way, but she's a very nervous, hyper woman."

The patient reports that the impression she has of her parents's relationship is that it was a good one. Her father was home all the time and she remembers few fights. Just before her father died he was hospitalized, at which time she and her mother moved to a smaller home, where they remained after his death. This was a dramatic change in their life and the patient no longer went to private school. Money was always a big problem—or at least her mother was always worrying about it.

The patient reports no emotional disorders in the family other than her feeling that her mother "really flipped out" several years after her father's death. At that time her mother was hospitalized for a couple of days for a hemorrhoidectomy, but the patient feels that this condition was a response to the tremendous stress she had been going through in getting a job, losing her husband, and raising a child by herself. She saw a psychiatrist for a while but told the patient that the only thing he did to help her was to prescribe tranquilizers. Her mother describes this as a depressed period but the patient says that it was more a case of hyperanxiety. She also says her mother had sleep and eating interference during that time, very much like her own this past spring. The patient reports no other close relatives.

She has had no serious illnesses or operations. The most serious thing she could think of was having her tonsils removed at sixteen. In high school and college she did a great deal of social drinking, "an awful lot," often getting so drunk she would throw up or pass out. She smoked marijuana occasionally, though she doesn't particularly like it. She has had no experience in therapy other than having seen a psychiatrist who simply prescribed medication for the sleep disturbance she suffered while in graduate school. She had had an abortion just prior to that, though it had upset her boyfriend far more than it had her.

The patient is very thin and slight, and has short black hair. She wears square metal-framed glasses. She came to her interview dressed in a blue T-shirt and shorts, walked on crutches, and was in considerable pain from her leg. She was very soft-spoken, though this clearly was an effect of the painkillers she was taking. Her face looked somewhat haggard though alert. She was feminine in appearance and all other behavioral features were well within normal limits. The interviewer felt very positively disposed to her and was aware of a very engaging interaction with her. She was both open and warm, though considerable sadness and depression showed through.

All mental status dimensions were within normal limits: memory, judgment, intelligence, concentration, capacity for abstraction, and orientation in all three spheres. The patient showed strong potential for reflection on her own motivation. Her affect was somewhat flat, a function of both depression and heavy painkillers. She reports no perceptual or thought disorders now or in the past, other than stating that during the period of severe depression *there were times when she "felt very unreal," when she just couldn't feel very alive.* Her only somatic complaints were sleep disorder and appetite disruption during the period of depression, and occasional difficulty in urinating. Her current concerns are that she is not going to be able to function when she leaves the hospital. She says she was very hopeful until her leg got worse, but that now she feels

hopeless and afraid of winding up a cripple. At the same time
she has a very sensitive approach to therapy and is anxious to
get to work.

Summary: The patient presents a depressive reaction that
continued unabated over a matter of months until in
desperation she took some seventy-five pills. The onset of the
depression is traced to her then impending graduation and the
need to take up a job and career. The patient has always
contained her latent depression by utilizing external structure: a boyfriend, a husband, a graduate school program. The
absence of a clearer structure and the uncertain requirements
of starting a new life was too much, especially when her more
adaptive obsessive defenses were failing her in her new career.
She felt too out of control in performing the therapeutic tasks
her job required.

The patient hints at a very lonely childhood, growing up
with a chronically ill, much older father, and without siblings.
Her mother seems well-intentioned but distant, and unable to
share with the patient her own pain at the loss of her husband.
The patient was frightened by her mother's late night sobbing
and seems to have never properly mourned the loss of her
father. This lack of mourning may have further complicated
the depressed core in both parents, who knew for years that
the father's gradually deteriorating condition would ultimately take his life. At the height of the patient's oedipal period her
parents were told, because of the father's health, to abstain
from sexual activity.

*Issues concerning the self—of strength, control, and
incompetence—seem to predominate.* These are evidenced in
recurrent dreams of falling and of being unable to locomote
when she wished. Throughout, the interviewer sensed the
patient's fear of feelings of powerlessness and loss of control.
The patient's willingness for therapy and her capacity for self-
examination and insight are prognostically hopeful signs.

Comment: This patient has lived *a secluded, lonely life
since early childhood, with feelings of failure and in-*

competence. She grew up with a mother whose mourning and depression frightened her; her childhood reveals *dreams of incompetence, powerlessness, and loss of control.* Her major satisfactions were for a time within her fantasy life, in talking to herself. Since age fifteen, she has had a *series of men to validate her self-esteem and to provide security.* She has thrived only in the structured situations lacking in her early life. *Her final reaction to her lonely pain was a depression* and a desire to quit through suicide, her attempt at which failed.

Diagnosis: Borderline Syndrome, Group IV.

Psychological Report: The following observations on the patient's psychological functioning can be made on the basis of her performance on several psychological tests given at the time of her hospitalization.

The patient's intelligence is that of a bright normal. Her cognitive performance was at times sporadic, though this stemmed more likely from problems of memory or attention than from the intrusion of disturbed thinking. Her Rorschach was characterized by thought that is highly constricted and quite conventional, with accompanying defenses of denial and avoidance. The contents of her percepts are most notable for their bland quality and absence of originality. The record indicates someone working hard to cover up quite painful and primitive representations. There are no overt signs of thought disorder on any of the patient's tests.

CASE 19

The patient graduated from high school in January 1974. For the next eight months she lived at home and *worked at several jobs,* including clerking in a warehouse and pumping gas. During this time she began to use marijuana and amphetamines frequently because they "made her feel good," although she denies any underlying depression. In September 1974, she enrolled simultaneously at a junior college, an academy of music, and an academy of arts, and planned to pursue studies in commercial art. After three days, however, she dropped out because she "couldn't draw," *and ran away* for three weeks. She then returned to Chicago to live with her parents and worked as a waitress. In March 1975, she went to Israel to work in a kibbutz for six months. While there, after drinking some wine, she *had an anxiety attack and ran away into the desert.* She was found by a search party and was sedated. The patient says this anxiety attack was the result of her being with the "wrong crowd," in which there were some sexual exploits and emotional problems, but she denies any sexual encounter at the time.

The patient returned to Chicago after this event, and again worked as a gas station attendant. In the summer of 1975 she began a college course in English composition but never completed it because she overdosed on Quaaludes and while under the influence of the drug smashed up her car. She was taken to a hospital, where she was unconscious for four days. This was a suicide attempt. She had obtained the Quaaludes from a "contact" she had at the gas station.

In September 1975, the patient enrolled at another college. *On the day classes were to begin, she overdosed* again on Quaaludes and was found unconscious by her roommate. She was taken to the hospital where she remained unconscious for one day in the ICU. When asked why she took the pills, the patient replied that she was tired of upsetting her parents with her behavior. After medical clearance, she was transferred to P&PI for psychiatric care. Prior to hospitalization, she had been in psychiatric treatment since age fourteen.

The patient, born and raised in suburban Chicago, is the youngest of three siblings. Her sister, twenty-seven, is married and works as a ward clerk in a hospital. This sister has been in treatment with a social worker due to "problems in relating to other people." She and her sister are very close despite an eight-year difference in age. Her brother, twenty-five, is married, lives in Chicago, and works as a salesman.

The parents have been married thirty years. The father is in good health except for a gastric ulcer. Very sensitive and emotional, he cries easily in emotionally stressful situations. The mother has hyperthyroidism. When the patient was young, before the mother's medical condition was diagnosed, she recalls that her mother was very nervous. "She was unbearable. She would scream and lock herself in a room for hours. She had thyroid trouble again a year ago but now with medication she's better. She is more mellow now." Recently the patient has gotten along better with both parents.

The patient's earliest memory is graduating from nursery school at age three. She laughs and recalls that the children all wore caps and gowns. She had a *recurrent frightening dream in which there were "bugs" crawling all over her room.* She recalls that after this dream she would cry and go to her parents' bedroom for the rest of the night. This behavior continued throughout grade school. She says she was a bed-wetter until age ten, but recalls playing normally with neighborhood children, their favorite game being kickball. She was a Girl Scout for one year. She also took piano lessons for a year.

The patient attended public grade school. She states that *she was always scared of going to school but the anxiety was nebulous and undefinable. Her academic performance has been erratic.* For example, she was an honors student in her junior year of high school, but *in her senior year she almost failed several courses.* Extracurricular activities included swimming, crafts, and spending time after school with her girlfriend. She says this girl has been her "best" friend since ninth grade. They were together all the time, earning the epithet *the Bobbsey twins.*

The patient had little experience dating boys. She had one relationship with a boy she met while working at the gas station. This lasted during her chaotic year following graduation. She had her first sexual intercourse with this boy, and says it was not especially good. The relationship ended in April because she "felt they were not meant for each other."

The patient is oriented; memory and intelligence are good. Affect during the interview was a continuous pleasant smile often inappropriate to the content of the material. *There is noticeable lack of insight into her impulsive behavior.* There is no psychotic thought process and no perceptual distortion. Suicidal ideation is not overt but is implied in the impulsive self-destructive behavior.

Comment: The patient exhibits several characteristics of a borderline personality with masked depression. Both parents seem to have been emotionally unavailable for long periods, causing developmental arrest and ego defects. She *exhibits hunger for a close relationship with an older woman,* as demonstrated by her love for her sister and her intimacy with her girlfriend. Impulse control is markedly impaired. She has a long history of *running away from home,* using this as a defense when her feelings became overwhelming. She is *aware of her impulse to run* but doesn't know why and can't control the impulse. The impulse to run seems to follow each attempt to separate from home and become independent. She can observe her behavior but the lack of understanding has resulted in guilt, shame, and subsequent depression.

From the secondary interview and the predischarge questionnaire it became clearer that the patient is *reticent about talking with people, stays alone, and feels that nobody cares for her. She has extremely low self-esteem. Her characteristic defense, especially evident during her first weeks of college, is to run away because she "can't be with people."* Thus she dated only a few times a year and is with a friend only once a week. She always feared school and as a child was *never interested in playing, preferring to be alone.* She also had night fears. *She feels separated from others and lonely,* which drives her to desperate attempts at suicide.

Psychological Tests Administered: Wechsler Adult Intelligence Test (5 Subtests); Draw-A-Person (DAP); Rorschach; Thematic Apperception Test (TAT); Minnesota Multiphasic Personality Inventory (MMPI).

During the three days of assessment, her mood, affect, and quality of interpersonal relations varied widely. Her mood ranged from detached to depressed to suspicious; *her affect from anxious to depressed to angry.* At times she was cooperative and sociable, at others withdrawn, oppositional, critical, and obstinate. Her psychomotor activity was sometimes normal and at other times slowed. *Thus there was an "in-and-out" quality in her relation to the examiner.* On most occasions, however, she maintained a guarded, somewhat aloof stance. There seemed to be no evidence of memory impairment, hallucinations or delusions, and she was oriented to person, place, and time.

The results of the assessment suggest that this patient fits the diagnostic category of borderline state. While only five subtests of the WAIS were given there are indications that she is currently functioning within the superior range of intelligence. However, there are indications of cognitive slippage on the WAIS which is probably attributable to her high degree of intrapsychic tension.

She seems to have a *poor self-concept and strong feelings of inadequacy.* She is dissatisfied with herself and cynical about her ability to resolve her emotional difficulties. Her frequent ruminations, self-doubting, and tenseness make it difficult for her to concentrate. These symptoms and feelings contribute to her irritability and impatience with others.

The patient's defenses seem quite rigid and when she faces stress there is a tendency toward fragmentation which results in episodic psychosis and irresponsible acting out. In most cases, however, the defenses are strong enough to avoid regression. The effort to avoid regression drains her psychic economy, however, and encroaches upon the autonomous ego-functions. Thus her ability to concentrate or to think creatively is somewhat diminished. She does appear to have several ego-strengths, however. It would seem that she can anticipate the consequences of her actions and is generally able to perceive without distortion.

Themes from the projective tests suggest that the patient felt *isolated and alienated from her family and society.* The largest conflict area appears to be with her mother. Here the feelings of isolation and alienation are profound. It would seem that there was much maternal deprivation during her early years and her running away from home and searching for different religious affiliations might be interpreted as a quest for the good, orally gratifying mother she never had. Her real mother is seen as ungiving, distant, and incapable of meeting her child's needs.

Finally there is *much conflict over her identity* as a maturing female. There has apparently not been sufficient identification with appropriate female objects for her to be comfortable with her feminine sexuality. Again her sense of isolation from her mother would be central in this area.

Summary: This nineteen-year-old woman presents symptoms of depression which seem to stem from long-standing feelings of isolation from her family in general and her mother in particular. Her defenses are quite rigid and there is a tendency toward fragmentation when under stress. There is much movement, both toward and movement away from people, as she searches for the good, orally satisfying object she never had. It should be noted that suicide is still a possibility with this patient and she should be monitored carefully.

Diagnosis: Borderline State with depression, Group IV.

Chapter 4
Differential Diagnosis

An area of doubt experienced by many clinical psychiatrists is the differential diagnosis of the borderline patient from those suffering from other syndromes, especially the schizophrenias. In fact some clinicians consider the borderline a form of latent or ambulatory schizophrenia. The term *latent* is an unfortunate misnomer because a patient either is or is not schizophrenic, but may or may not be overtly or latently psychotic. Among the psychoses there are a variety of conditions other than schizophrenia: manic-depressive, toxic, infectious, traumatic, arteriosclerotic, senile, etc.

The borderline syndrome as a diagnostic category occupies an area between the neuroses and the psychoses. Within specific individuals, it may abut on or approach one or the other of these poles, and oscillation between them is not uncommon. Hence the term *stable instability*. The question of a psychiatric spectrum of continuities, as contrasted with separately defined and discrete entities, is still moot in the literature. In our original research monograph, we assumed that so much had been written about neuroses, personality and character disorders, and the various forms of psychopathy and psychoses that repetition was unnecessary, but we soon found that critics continually confused the borderline with other diagnostic entities. We feel, therefore, that it is important to present from our material case examples that demonstrate differentiation.

Many schizophrenics seem to have elevated, excited moods resembling mania. Others are depressed and suicidal, although this mood should be discriminated from anhedonia. We therefore hedge in labeling them, diagnosing them as neither schizophrenic nor manic-depressive but schizo-active. There is no evidence from the clinical data that the thought disorders of both are identical, but about 20 percent of manic depressives do have some form of thought disorder—in our opinion quite different from the schizophrenic—and their depressions are different from the borderline.

There has been an attempt to designate acute schizophrenia, involving one or several psychotic breakdowns, as a disease different from slowly progressive, chronic schizophrenia. This eventually leads to what is called the *schizophrenic spectrum* (including the borderline), a psychiatric mishmash in the families of index subjects. Neurotic or psychopathological traits in the families or siblings of index subjects might well be detected in anyone. Diagnosis and classification would have to backtrack if spectrum concepts have any validity as genetic markers, and specific syndromes would require identification instead of the fragile omnibus of "sick families." Also, the supposed absence of spectrum diagnoses for relatives of acute schizophrenic index cases is no indication that the acute are genetically unrelated to the other types. Clinicians know that one or several acute breakdowns may precede the development of a chronic and often irreversible course.

There are changing manifestations to be found in all psychiatric disorders: conversion hysteria, mania, catatonia, hebephrenia, etc. But in certain cases, among them the borderline patients, what seems most prominent is a restricted and constricted character. It is this that led us to our original study.

What seems clear is that schizophrenia is a system diagnosable by the presence of biopsychosocial parts inefficiently controlled or regulated by an organizational principle. Specific preparedness, derived from biogenetic factors, is sensitive to a wide variety of precipitating stimuli which we cannot differentiate into internal and external. Prior to the overt onset, prediction is almost impossible from the premorbid state. Even after a psychotic break or the recognition of thought disorder in a quiescent schizophrenic, prediction of future attacks is very difficult.

What we can state is that when the schizophrenic organization weakens or breaks we may observe two classes of symptom, as originally formulated by Hughlings Jackson. One is the loss of functional control determined by the absence of high-level thinking and feeling. These weak or deficient parts often cannot be altered by compensatory functions. The other class of symptom is the presence of old functions, always alive but repressed or controlled, revived by the absence or weakness of regulation.

Borderline patients do not present with first-rank Schneiderian symptoms. Furthermore they reveal no lowered level of consciousness, no delusions, hallucinations, abnormal mobility, or incoherent thinking. Neither do we see in the borderline Shakow's (1971) disturbance in generalized set, the presence of segmental set, or the affective or cognitive disturbances described by him.

OVERALL CHARACTERISTICS
OF THE BORDERLINE SYNDROME

Four basic facts are derived from the total analysis of the data in the ego-functions framework: (1) Expressed more or less directly to a variety of targets, *anger* seems to constitute the main or only affect the borderline patient experiences. (2) The borderline patient is characterized by a *defect in his affectional relationships*. These are anaclitic, dependent, or complementary, but rarely reciprocal. (3) *Indications of consistent self-identity are absent*, a fact which seems linked to the lack of affectional relationship and consistency, with anger at closeness. (4) This vacillating behavior is associated with *a confused view of the self*—"as if I were watching myself playing a role."

CHARACTERISTICS OF THE FOUR SUBGROUPS (1968 CASES)

Group I: *The Psychotic Border*
1. Behavior inappropriate, nonadaptive toward other humans
2. Self-identity, and reality sense deficient
3. Negative behavior toward others expressed by angry eruptions in an impulsive manner
4. Depression

Group II: *The Core Borderline Syndrome*
1. Vacillating involvement with others, confusing them by positive and negative acting
2. Anger acted out
3. Depression when not acting angrily
4. Self-identity not consistent

Group III: *The Adaptive, Affectless, As-if Person*
1. Behavior adaptive, appropriate
2. Complementary relationships with no sense of self-identity
3. Little positive affect, spontaneity lacking
4. Defenses of withdrawal and intellectualization

Group IV: *The Border with the Neuroses*
1. Anaclitic depression often intense
2. Anxiety increased by close relations to maternal figures
3. Resemblance to neurotic, narcissistic character

SOCIAL CHARACTERISTICS OF THE ORIGINAL BORDERLINE CASES

	Number	Percent
Sex	51	100
Male	28	55
Female	23	45

	Number	*Percent*
Age	51	100
Less than 30 years	39	76
30 years or older	12	24
Race	51	100
White	46	90
Negro	5	10
Religion	51	100
Protestant	17	33
Catholic	27	53
Jewish	6	12
Other	1	02
Marital Status	51	100
Single (never married)	29	57
Married (living with spouse)	13	25
Married (separated)	7	14
Divorced	2	04
Admission to Hospital	51	100
Voluntary	39	76
Committed	12	24

PRECIPITANTS TO HOSPITALIZATION OF THE BORDERLINE

	Total Cases: 51
Depression without specific suicide attempt or ideation	5
Suicidal ideation	5
Attempted suicide	4
Impulse eruption; inability to regulate aggression	2
Anxiety (acute and/or diffuse)	5
Phobias	4
Alcohol and/or drugs	4
Ritualistic compulsive behavior	2
Somatization	3
Disorders of thinking and association	3
Combination of above	11
Other	3

The method of our recent research consisted of taping interviews with all newly admitted young adults, interviews conducted by a senior psychiatrist with no knowledge of the patient's clinical history or diagnosis. Later each subject was rated by three investigators who listened to the tapes together and rated them according to the following Trait Inventory.

SCHIZOPHRENIA TRAIT INVENTORY
(Check the highest appropriate number)
 I. *Language Problems*
    0. Well modulated, no impairment in syntax
    1. Mild paucity of thoughts or reduced richness in language
    2. Language well modulated in reference to impersonal things, but occasionally impaired when referring to the self or threatening the self
    3. Circumstantiality
       Literalness
       Concreteness
    4. Anithetical meanings manifested
    5. Autistic intrusions
       Predicate identifications
       Loosening of associations
       Blocking
    6. Perseverations
       Echolalia
       Neologisms
       Incoherence
 II. *Anxiety*
    0. Normal alertness
    1. Episodes of apprehension
    2. Episodes of panic
    3. Episodes of dread of self-dissolution and/or world destruction fantasies
    4. Episodes of feeling the world has already ended
    5. Continuous feelings of dread (reportable)
    6. Catatonic excitement

III. *Pleasure*
  0. Pleasure in accordance with external events
  1. Occasional but rare pleasure in accordance with external events
  2. Occasional pleasure but discordant with external events
  3. Lack of humor
  4. No convincing report of ever having fun
  5. No joy, exuberance, or knowledge of shared happiness
  6. Constant sadness or boredom
IV. *Unintegrated Self* (these are states of being)
  0. Well-differentiated roles
     Stable sense of self
  1. Shifting of roles within a situation or from situation to situation that is poorly modulated
     Identity felt as a function of role situation
     Grossness of role models i.e., awkwardness or "as if" quality to various roles
     Adoption of inappropriate roles to external requirements
     Single role from situation to situation
  2. Instances of hypochondriasis or psychosomatic disturbances
     Disorders of volition
  3. Splits in viewing the self
     Dress or grooming consistent except for a circumscribed part
  4. Inability to differentiate or assess other people's roles or moods
     Pronounced passive compliance
     Severe negativism
     Extreme grandiosity
  5. Dysynchrony of body parts
     Posturing
     Aberrations in body self such as body-image distortions, somatic delusions, bizarre hypochondriasis
     Derealization
     Depersonalization

6. Feelings or delusions of influence
   Persecutory or erotic delusions
   Auditory hallucinations where the sounds or voices are identified as a collective with certain aims
   Loss of self such as in command automatisms or catatonic stupor

V. *Inconsistency-Consistency Axis*

A. Thinking

0. Logical and appropriate
1. Circumstantiality—i.e., thoughts not directly related to conclusions
2. Ambivalence of thought in which contrary thoughts exist simultaneously without a feeling of paradox or an attempt to unify or synthesize
3. Thoughts inconsistent with external demands—i.e., outside information does not revise or change a set.
   Obsessions to delusions
   Maintenance of a rigid internal set
   Hypermnesia or a rigid adherence to detail, though the excess information is extraneous to complete the thought
   Recurrence of same theme to perseveration
   Confabulations
   Rigid reliance on external structure for directing thinking
4. Thoughts and affect not related
   One thought evoking a number of affects
   One affect manifested through different emotionally toned themes
5. Thoughts not related with one another in socially consensual ways.
   Linkage awry
6. Amorphous

B. Affect (does not include anxiety or dread)

0. Affect consistent with reality
1. Affect changeable during the same thoughts
2. Affect shifting rapidly in intensity
3. Ambivalence of affect toward the same object existing simultaneously without a feeling of paradox

4. Affect not congruent with the situation
5. Flatness or maintenance of a singular affect as in the angry paranoid
6. Uncontrolled affects such as mindless rages
   Affects observed not consistent with affect reported
C. Perception
0. Realistic
1. Denial of percepts or parts of percepts
2. Behavior or affect not congruent with either the perception or stimuli of the outer world—e.g., feeling menaced by some unknown force yet soliciting attention
3. Feeling of some inexplicable change in the perception of the outer world
4. Hyperconsistency—Singular perception toward all people (part-object) either neutral, erotically (as in erotomanic), or hostilely as in a persecutory delusion
5. Same people viewed quite differently sequentially without a sense of paradox
   Confusion of one person with another or of self and another
6. Distorted perception of inanimate objects
   Total loss of reality testing such as in a catatonic excitement

The techniques available for diagnoses and differential diagnoses include primarily the clinical psychiatric interview, behavior on the hospital nursing unit, family constellation, psychological tests, type of drug use, and follow-up. In describing the fourteen new borderline cases (chapter 3), we have *italicized the core stable elements* characterizing the syndrome, but many peripheral characteristics remain, contributing to individual differences. These are based on individual life experiences, defenses, substitute fulfillment of needs (drugs, alcohol), conflict over anger (anorexia), passivity ("as if"), depression with suicidal impulses, and obsessive compulsive behavior. These *peripheral characteristics* have a tendency to shift throughout life (Maddi 1968).

The intermingling of core, peripheral, and precipitating factors requires that the differential diagnosis include other personality disorders (narcissism, antisocial personality, drug abuse, and alcoholism), depressive neuroses, schizoaffective and pseudoneurotic schizophrenias. In fact the differentiation extends throughout the entire range of neurotic, personality, and psychotic disorders.

Our methodology not only enabled us to study young, early-break schizophrenias, but included nonschizophrenic hospitalized patients serving as controls. Some of them could be spinned off as subjects for investigation as separate entities, for example, anorexias, obesities, young depressions. For our purposes we were able to extract fourteen new cases of the borderline syndrome. These are described in detail in chapter 3, and core and peripheral symptoms are detailed. The special methodological advantage is that this sample was in no way preselected.

After the ratings were made the results were recorded on a coding sheet for computer analysis and a graphic profile of the seven large categories (I, II, III, IV, VA, VB, and VC) of the Schizophrenia Trait Inventory was drawn. We present a composite comparison of the fourteen borderline cases with the diagnoses schizophrenics (Fig. 1).

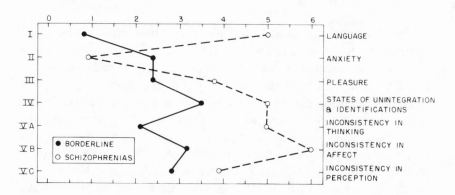

Figure 1

1a: Schizophrenia

Beck (1964) contrasts schizophrenia with the borderline, terming the latter a sanctuary type which shows affective lability and some subtle associative disintegration. These patients "know" the world of reality; they live at an even tempo and on the surface seem unruffled. Language is free from confusion; there is little disorganization of thinking, and errors of judgment are avoided. On the negative side are concrete thinking, hypersensitivity, poverty of fantasy, self-depreciation, self-absorption, and restrictive and constrictive defenses.

Artiss (1966) described the schizophrenic's behavior operationally as (1) "too much" or "too little," (2) deficient in social skills, and (3) odd and idiosyncratic in use of language which seemingly bids for deviance. Artiss summarizes: "The schizophrenic's quandary results from a relative deficit in the connotative aspects of language." The schizophrenic rejects novelty and perseverates the old.

In summary, we can state that the borderline patient does not have, as has the schizophrenic, the following traits: (1) disturbances in intellectual associational processes, (2) autistic or regressive thinking, (3) characteristic family with "pseudomutuality" or "skewing," (4) delusions or hallucinations, (5) deficit in connotative aspects of language.

Nevertheless the patients in Group I reveal behaviors which are negative and inappropriate toward their environment, indicating a state "close to disintegration." If psychotic disintegration does occur it is transient, sometimes for only a few hours. On this basis Frosch (1964) terms them *psychotic characters*.

The transient behaviors labeled psychotic differ from those observed in schizophrenic psychoses. They seem to be induced by quantities of rage unmanageable by the deficient defensive functions of the ego.

The following case report, based on two interviews three years apart, exemplifies schizophrenia.

CASE 20

This is the first P&PI admission for a twenty-three-year-old white married male whose chief complaints were: "I am overly sensitive," "I want others to be as sensitive as I am," "I don't know why I'm here," and "The trouble started because I was too proud."

The patient was admitted April 27, 1971, having been referred by his stepfather following "an acute paranoid eruption with yelling and posturing." The present break was preceded by a trip with the patient's wife and a friend. While there, the patient was "rejected" by the friend and he and his wife returned alone. When home he and his wife took drugs and got along for a while, but their relationship was punctuated with periodic outbursts of jealousy accompanied by posturing. A few days prior to admission, the patient returned to Chicago, his boyhood home, to seek a divorce. While staying with his parents he had several outbursts, which necessitated his admission. The patient has a history of paranoid episodes throughout his marriage of ten months. He and his wife had lived together prior to their marriage for about four years without any incident of this magnitude.

The patient, an only child, was born in 1947. His father and mother were divorced when he was six. He says he did not know his father well until some years later, at which time he came to like him very much as a person. He describes his mother as overprotective and doting. Shortly after the divorce she remarried; he had a positive reaction to his stepfather, especially because he "got a lot of presents."

His earliest childhood memory is of standing on the balcony of his parents' apartment looking out over the lake. He described this as a "pleasant experience" but made no other comment. He did well in school and always had a lot of friends. He enjoyed growing up. Home life was calm and sedate; his mother and stepfather never fought and were always kind to him. He enjoyed sports and outdoor activities while in school and was able to take frequent camping trips. He left home at age eighteen to attend university. There he majored in English and wrote many stories and poems. His aspiration was to become a writer. While in college he joined a fraternity and had many good times with other students. He also met his future wife and began living with her. To him she was the one woman he "could not live without."

Upon graduation he taught English to avoid military service. He did not want to teach and did not like it at all. At that time he lived with another teacher—his fiancee was still attending college—with whom he supposedly had a "sado-masochistic relationship."

During this time he apparently tried and failed to get some of his writings published. He does not much like to talk about this. At the end of the schoolyear he decided that he "could no longer live without his lover and they were married. He says that marriage was "her idea."

Sometime either before or after marriage (this is not clear), he took several trips with a group. On one particular outing the group climbed Mt. Rainier. He "knew," he said, that everyone else in the group was using oxygen on the way up but they did not offer him any. He felt bad about this at first but then decided he "didn't care." He says that he was "too proud" to ask for oxygen and that they didn't give him any until they reached the peak, by which time he apparently needed it badly. He apparently had several outbursts during the rest of the trip, which caused his companions to ask him to go home early. He traces all of his troubles to this episode.

He claims to be a very sensitive person and gets very upset when others around him do not appreciate his sensitivity or are not themselves sensitive. When asked which people in particular this applied to, he answered, "the whole country."

He is cleanshaven and well-dressed, has tousled hair of moderate length, and is generally neatly groomed. His facies bespeak depression. He exhibits very unusual motor posing at all times except when engaged in playing pingpong. He walks up and down while in the lounge. The posing usually involves head and hands, sometimes the whole body. He will be walking along and suddenly stop, look down, and hold the pose for fifteen to twenty seconds. On two occasions the patient seemed quite detached and wandered about. He is subdued and quiet throughout the interviews and makes no outbursts.

His memory has been difficult to evaluate, because he does not cooperate in recalling past events. His recent memory is good, however; he recalls all events since admission. He is well oriented, but his judgment is cloudy—full of doubts about what to do in any given situation. He will take both sides of any issue presented rather than making a choice. He is very intelligent, has read widely, and can recall stories in minute detail, providing a running critique and interpretation. He speaks continually in parables and proverbs appropriate to the point being discussed, and he has a vivid imagination.

The nurse's notes indicate occasional violent episodes or explosions of rage, seemingly triggered by violence on the ward or on TV. These episodes cease as suddenly as they begin, lasting only a few seconds. At other times the patient is depressed and refuses to talk. When depressed he will wander to and fro on the unit. Generally he lacks any sustained expressions of joy and feeling. One feels depressed talking with him. Affect is frequently inappropriate to the situation. For instance, everyone else will be laughing or hollering and he will remain uninvolved.

His thoughts are quite poorly connected and he changes topics quite suddenly and without warning. He responds well to guiding of thoughts by others; though some of his thoughts are complete, others are left hanging and must be guided to completion. He has no language abnormalities but seems preoccupied with references to himself. His perceptions do not appear on the surface to be distorted, at least at present. He gives no history of hallucinations or other distortions, except perhaps of hypersensitivity to all events about him. He seems well grounded in reality, but seems to be concealing a good deal with regard to his past and present perceptions.

He reports trouble sleeping in the past; sometimes staying awake three or four days at a time. He has ideas of grandeur, as revealed by his remark about the "whole country" being insensitive. At first he seemed afraid of being "locked up." This fear was manifested not as an obvious anxiety reaction, but instead more subtly with sweaty palms (his hands were dripping wet at the first interview). Since admission he seems gradually less and less afraid and the physical symptoms have disappeared. He remarked to the nurses on occasion that his wife had "demasculinized" him. When asked to explain this he would either refuse outright or evade the question.

Affective disturbances—The patient generally displays little or no emotion either appropriate or inappropriate to the situation. He speaks of himself as "controlled"—probably meaning not showing his inward rage. He speaks very slowly and deliberately and in a quiet voice—making his listener almost drowsy at times. That emoion is occurring is evidenced by the frequent tensing of his muscles and the excessive sweating of his palms.

Associative looseness—As mentioned before, the patient's thoughts were frequently unconnected and incomplete, frequently plunging from one subject straight into the middle of another.

Autistic thinking—The patient seems preoccupied with his own "sensitive" reactions and feelings.

Ambivalence—The patient displays considerable vacillation when asked for a judgment or conclusion on anything. If he seems to have taken one viewpoint on a subject, such as saying he prefers the East Coast as a place to live, and the interviewer says "Oh, so you like living in New Hampshire?" the patient will suddenly reverse himself with: "I suppose it's not where I belong; I like the Midwest better." He does not seem to care about most matters, except those in which he is directly involved (such as playing pingpong).

Comment: The patient has always been dependent on his mother and yet withdraws into loneliness and sadness, with crying or angry shouting. He becomes anxious when he tries to do too much and has a fleeting fear of insanity. Failure interferes with his feeling like God. His writing is confused, a "destructive analysis of my mind." His thoughts become linked together and his identity as a person in college and in the world is confused. He writes in symbols and has delusions

of grandeur. He perceives internal signals in his body and
laughs inappropriately.

Three years later, on his second admission, he still had
delusions of influence; his thoughts were not related in
socially consensual ways; his affect was intense anger with
the situation, and his view of people shifted rapidly at
different times. He was quite disorganized.

1b: Pseudoneurotic Schizophrenia

Since Hoch and Polatin described this entity (1949), little
further information has been published regarding its
characteristics. The three generalities—pananxiety, pansex-
uality and panneurosis—have been of little help in diagnosing
or understanding the condition, except after a psychosis has
developed. The patients to whom this diagnosis is applied
become psychotic less often than other schizophrenics. At
some time in the course of their illness, prior to the
development of an overt schizophrenic psychosis, they may be
mistaken for borderline cases.

Weingarten and Korn (1967) have reported on ten
pseudoneurotic schizophrenics who comprise 11 percent of
eighty-seven patients studied by a variety of psychological
tests. They report the following results: (1) good social facade,
appropriate behavior, and well-kept appearance; (2)
successful academic and occupational attainment; (3) underlying thought disorder involving primary-process thinking; (4) forced or contrived affectional responsiveness; (5)
unabating states of tension, constant turmoil; (6) ego-syntonic
acceptance of thought disorder, ego-alien reaction to social
maladjustment or academic failure; and (7) profuse, unintegrated neurotic and psychotic defenses.

These patients, when decompensating into a psychosis
because of external stress, internal tensions, or injudicious
reconstructive therapy, cannot be differentiated from other
schizophrenics.

2: Depression

CASE 21

The patient is a twenty-two-year-old married Jewish woman admitted to P&PI for her fifth psychiatric hospitalization. "Depression. I feel I have no place to turn. My doctor gave me an alternative of hospitalization."

The patient describes how she has been depressed, with sadness, loss of appetite, and suicidal thoughts for three months. She recognizes several external stresses, including unhappiness with her marriage of three years. She says she has gotten no sexual satisfaction from this marriage. She also feels that she has a very poor relationship with her parents. She has been despondent and cranky, and has recently lacked confidence in herself. She has been in therapy for several months and feels her depression was brought on by the therapy: "We have been hitting tender spots and it's left all in my mind." Several weeks ago the patient had an impulse to drive her car into a wall. Several nights before admission she ingested ten minor tranquilizers in order to commit suicide but "they weren't strong enough." She was found sleeping in the kitchen by her husband. No medical treatment was indicated. She has had decreased appetite and has lost a few pounds in the past week.

She was the oldest of six children. The next in age was two years younger and mentally retarded. She describes how this child was treated like a doll by the family and was put in an institution at three years of age. The next in age was six years younger than the patient, the other three eight, ten, and twelve years younger. She describes her early years as fairly happy. Her father she describes as fairly passive, and she feels very much like him. Her mother is a vindictive woman who is easily hurt and can't take criticism. The patient's earliest memory is of having pneumonia at the age of three and being in the hospital. After that her parents gave her her choice of going to either California or Florida to recuperate. She describes a dream which was recurrent at about the time she was eleven: a tank was rolling down the hill and she felt that it might roll over her. She got along well in school and had many friends. Her grades were above average. Her parents always told her that she was smarter than her grades indicated. Her menarche was at thirteen years of age, and she had been told about it ahead of time by her mother and by her physician. She was not greatly surprised, nor was she happy about it. Her periods were unusually long and heavy, lasting eight days of heavy flow. She was the first person in her group of friends to begin to menstruate. She had no close girlfriend during her early adolescence but did have a group of three to four girlfriends. However, later in adolescence, this group broke up as in high school she began to date older men, and her friends were either "wild" or not interested in dating at all. She describes herself as very moody and blue during her high school years. She went to college and there met her future husband. He was the first man with whom she had sexual intercourse. She dropped out of college after two years, and worked to let her husband finish his Ph.D. She has worked since, even though he is now employed. They have had no children because they don't want any. She added that she needs her job to support her therapy.

The patient is an attractive woman who appeared poised and related appropriately throughout the interview. She acted somewhat seductively and had a somewhat constricted range of affect. She was attractively dressed and groomed.

She was well oriented in all spheres. Her memory, both recent and remote, was intact, as were her judgment and intelligence. Her affect was somewhat constricted but not depressive. She was mildly histrionic, pleasant, and seductive. Her thoughts were logical and goal oriented and there was no evidence of any psychotic disorder. She interpreted proverbs abstractly. She currently had suicidal ideation but was not actively suicidal or homicidal.

The *psychological test protocols* suggested a depressed personality. Anxiety, particularly overaggressive urges, was prominent and could produce disruption in adaptive efforts. Some confusional experiences were thus likely. There did not appear to be any thought disorder that would suggest schizophrenic pathology. Suicidal potential was indicated. A general dysphoria—a depression—was diagnosed.

Full-scale IQ was 112 (bright normal), verbal IQ 108 (average), performance IQ 116 (bright normal).

Follow-up two years later revealed that the patient had suffered a relapse a year after discharge, having become depressed while pregnant, and returned to the hospital for a short time. The patient now enjoys life and has fun, competent both as a mother and in her work. She considers that she has been helped a great deal. "I am now able to do everything and raise a family."

Diagnosis: Depression, probably with manic elements to appear more severely later.

Since last tested psychologically (three years ago), she has come much more in contact with her feelings, with conflicts no longer intruding so much on her thinking and language. There is consideradly less disruptive anxiety, and no evidence of thought disorder. She remains predominantly focused on herself, so that she does not go out of her way to make her thinking clear or explicit to the examiner. Her major concerns are infantile and narcissistic. There is some suggestion that her earlier conflicting and complex emotional activity has left as a vestige an unorganized sense of internal tension. Within her characterological style, however, she is able to cope with these tensions.

In one factor of each of three borderline patient groups *depression* was observed. Only in Group III, characterized by adaptation and absence of affect, was depression not characteristic. Contrary to the dynamic stereotype that depression is always the obverse of hostility, the two were sometimes correlated in a single factor. In factor II of Group I, depression was associated with verbally and behaviorally expressed anger. In factor I of Group II, depression was positively correlated with negative behaviors and anger. On the other hand, depression was associated with anxiety in factor II of Group IV. Actually the depressed appearance, which is basically the effect of loneliness (except in Group IV), contributes the most significant problem in differential diagnosis.

We turn back to review our studies in the *Phenomena of Depression* (Grinker et al. 1961) to compare the factors developed in that research. There was no similarity with the borderline in the factors of the pilot study. For example in factor A depression was associated with guilt and remorse, which are not seen in any borderline. Factor B was involved with hopeful attachment to the external world, with the idea that supplies and gratification were due these patients. These same criteria were characteristic of "feelings and concerns" in factor II of the main study. In this study, "feelings and concerns" (factor IV), which were essentially anxiety, and factor V, which included traits of "unloved, clinging, angry" attempts to force others to give, were in combination, as in factor II of Group IV borderline. In the study of "outward behaviors" in depression, the isolation and withdrawal of factor I was like factor I of Group III borderline; factor I, including clinging, ingratiating behavior, was like Group IV of the borderline. The combination factor patterns in the depression study were not similar to any of the borderline categories.

In general it can be stated that although depression as an affect is found in several of the borderline categories it does not correspond with that seen in the depressive syndrome. The borderline depression is a feeling of loneliness and isolation. The exception is Group IV (borderline on the neurotic) which is similar to the neurotic anaclitic depressive syndrome in which there is a great hunger for dependent gratification.

3: Personality Disorders

CASE 22

This is a seventeen-year-old single Jewish female. The patient has been feeling very tense and anxious and has not been able to attain her goals.

Much of the present illness can be dated to her final semester in high school, although relevant events go back even farther. She was an excellent student in high school, attaining almost straight A's, and she intended to graduate in only three years. During her final semester, however, her grades fell severely to C's and D's. She claims that she just lost interest in schoolwork but that she maintained a good relationship with most of her teachers, all of whom knew that she was a very good student. Although she did graduate at the end of the semester, it was in some doubt all the time. During her final year she had worked part-time in a nursing home and decided that she wanted to go into nursing. Since this would require one year of regular college, she wanted to go to the local university. She says that because her graduation was in some doubt she was unable to apply for September admission. Instead, after graduation she began to work full-time over the summer and went to a state college at night while living at home.

During July she suddenly decided to run away. She denies having any specific reason for this at that time. The only thing she mentioned was that she was not quite as happy in her then current nursing home job, which was at a public nursing home, as she had been in her previous job, which was at a private nursing home. She flew West and stayed in a commune for one night and then went to Sacramento, where she stayed in a hotel for a few days. She relates the experience of walking past several bars near the hotel and feeling, "My God, what is Daddy's little girl doing here?" and then going to the police station and asking for a ride back to her hotel. The police asked her name and age and gave her the ride. She would have liked the police to discover that she was a runaway and was disappointed they did not. She then went to Oklahoma City and stayed with an aunt and uncle. They said she could stay there as long as she wanted. However, only one week after she had left home, she felt she could go home and that things would get much better.

After returning home she found the situation unimproved. Her parents and relatives seemed extra courteous and polite toward her and she was forced to put up a facade of happiness and "bullshit" them (a phrase she uses often when unable to communicate or be understood). She mentioned several times that "when I can't bullshit or lie there is nothing left to do." Shortly after her return from her one-week trip to the West Coast, her father suggested she seek psychiatric help. She resisted at that time but finally in September began seeing a psychiatrist on an outpatient basis for approximately eight sessions prior to her admission.

The weekend before Thanksgiving of this year her aunt and uncle were expected to come in for a visit; the day before this the patient cut her wrist by making several superficial horizontal cuts with her manicure scissors. There was only a slight amount of bleeding and she was able to stop it quite easily. She called her doctor to discuss it with him and he told her that if she did this again, she would probably have to be hospitalized. The patient does not know why she cut her wrist a second time, but this time her father noticed and called the doctor, who suggested she be hospitalized the day after Thanksgiving. In the meantime there was a family meeting attended by both parents, her sister, her brother, and herself. According to the patient, many things were discussed and some feelings were hurt but she felt better for a while after this meeting. However, on Thanksgiving Day relatives came over and she again felt the need to put up a facade. Once again she cut her wrist and this time her arm and shoulder as well, though again only superficially.

The patient's father is described as a nervous and frustrated person who in 1965 had a nervous breakdown. She states that because of this the family atmosphere was very tense, that everybody had to be extremely quiet, avoiding conversations, not answering phone calls, and so on, in deference to her father. This general family situation has existed for as long as she can remember, although her father has with psychiatric help improved quite a bit. She feels that he is stable now and will not crack up again. He sees his psychiatrist only occasionally. He is described as being a hot-and-cold in-dividual, very inconsistent. At one moment he seems warm and eager to discuss her problems; the next moment, cold, callous, and intolerant toward her. He has been financially successful only recently, having lately achieved moderate success and security. She recalls an incident, about two years after his nervous breakdown, in which she went into the school bathroom and banged her arm against the wall in an attempt to fracture it. She felt that this could arouse her father from his state of depression. She failed, however, to break her arm and only bruised it severely. Her father came to the school and was very angry and took her home. A few weeks later, however, she tripped and broke her arm accidentally.

When asked about her mother, the patient said, "I've never really thought about her before." She offers no concrete description of her. She did mention that her mother became ill in 1960 and was hospitalized with nephritis for several months. During that time the patient and her sister had to assume many of the household duties. Upon recovering, the mother had to start working and has done so since. The relationship between her mother and her father she describes as being fairly good.

She has one older sister, age twenty-one, a student at the local university. The patient was not close to this sister until recently, when they began discussing things together. There was a period of about one year and a half during which they did not speak at all. This began after her sister spent the weekend at home with a boyfriend while she was pinned to another boy. The two spent the whole weekend in the bedroom, which surprised the patient quite a bit. An older brother is twenty-four, and she says her relationship with him has not been close either. Recently he has called a few times to find out about her and this has surprised her. She remembers that her father beat him severely several times as a child. Her reaction to this was generally one of fright. Sometimes she was angry at her brother for upsetting the father and thereby getting all the kids in trouble; at other times she felt very sympathetic toward him.

When asked about her earliest memories, she came up with two incidents of being hurt—once when she was pushed down the stairs by her brother, and another time when her toe got caught in the spokes of her bicycle. She also recalled an incident of playing with some friends and accidentally breaking her parents' bed. Her parents were very mad at first and punished her for a short time, but then all was forgotten. This seemed the general pattern of punishment for her. There were no deaths or separations during her childhood.

She has several close friends at present and has never had any difficulty establishing relationships. However, she did say that she felt many people were not sincere and truthful. Several people phoned her when she was in the hospital, including her brother and several teachers, which surprised her quite a bit. With the exception of her father's there are no mental disturbances in the family. She has had no surgery and denies any significant medical illnesses. She has smoked marijuana and drinks occasionally but takes no medication.

At each of three interviews the patient was casually dressed, with her shirt hanging out. She is moderately obese and walks with a peculiar rapid shuffle, usually holding her face down. Throughout the sessions she appeared extremely agitated; smoked continuously through the first session but not the final two. She changed position frequently, running her hands through her hair or rubbing her hands together much of the time. She is intelligent, interesting, perceptive, and capable of arousing empathy—in general, likable. She remained very anxious through the second and third sessions. I informed her that I was a resident, something I assumed she already knew. During the third interview, she mentioned that prior to my beginning the diagnostic evaluation, the director had asked her if she minded being interviewed by a staff member. She had replied, "They don't mean anything to me and I don't mean anything to them, and therefore I don't care."

The patient's memory, orientation, judgment, intelligence, concentration, and abstraction ability all appear closely intact and I did not test them specifically. Her affect and thought processes seemed entirely normal. She mentioned that she prefers to remain awake most of the night since she has been in the hospital, even though she does get along well with the other patients. She tries to sleep during the day, and has not asked for any sleep medication. She had not been sleeping well at home either. There is no evidence of any perceptual distortions or delusions. She denies any suicidal or homicidal intent, pointing out that she did not cut herself deeply.

The patient is experiencing a desire to be protected and closely attended to by her father. She admits to strong feelings of affection for him and to the longing to have a "real father." It seems probable that her father has shown the ability to be a strong, effective influence in her life, yet because of his own problems has suffered from extreme tension and depression. As an adolescent the patient is also faced with the task of gaining some independence from her parents, and this is a source of conflict leading to her own frustration and depression. The family atmosphere has never presented a proper outlet for the discharge of anger; in fact, she had to internalize her anger because of the presumed disastrous effects it would have on her father's mental state. The only way to discharge the tension and gain needed attention was to direct her anger against herself. Indeed, the patient when asked about her earliest childhood memories cited two incidents in which she was physically harmed. Little is known about the mother, but it might be postulated that she did not adequately meet her daughter's needs in infancy, which later manifested itself in infantile behavior, a type of behavior indicating dependency and urgency of demands. Both the attempt to break her own arm and the recent wrist cutting are indicative of this. Finally, there appears to be a good deal of anxiety over the separation that would take place if she went away to college. This tension was somewhat relieved by her suddenly doing poorly in school.

Diagnosis: Narcissistic neurosis.

The psychological tests are consistent with a self-centered young girl prone to act out conflicts with a predominantly oral-aggressive content. An arbitrary quality to her interpersonal relationships, a certain recklessness and low anxiety tolerance in an otherwise well-endowed girl suggests a narcissistic character.

Full-scale IQ is 122, verbal IQ 129, performance IQ 111.

Character disorders are relatively stable, ego-syntonic adaptations to a field of process in conflict. Character represents an adaptive synthesis. Only when this state of equilibrium breaks down does an ego-alien and distressful *psychoneurosis* develop. There are many nuances of character, some of which have been given such names as *neurotic, erotic, compulsive, narcissistic,* and *psychopathic,* and many others defined according to their predominating type of behavior.

In many psychiatric centers what corresponds to the borderline syndrome is diagnosed as chronic severe personality or character disorder. Similar to chronic undifferentiated schizophrenia, this vague item in our nosological classification is used not only because the borderline syndrome has not been defined and differentiated but also because it does not exist in our nosological classification.

Unlike the temporary disintegrations, the defenses of the borderline person are characterological and correspond to those employed by psychoneurotics. This is the borderline's adaptive overlay acquired over many years; the defenses become ego-syntonic. They probably become intensified as the first reaction to specific strains, especially the threat of closeness. For this reason withdrawal, intellectualization, and denial are so frequent—techniques that increase interpersonal distance.

During their hospital stay so little stress impinged on these patients that extraordinary coping strategies were not necessary. Only in the period between decision for discharge and actual discharge did the patients show stress responses.

On the other hand, sexual acting out and alcoholic excesses occurred on passes away from the hospital. These were easily detected and reported within our behavioral observations. They may have constituted defenses against anxiety and/or substitute gratification without the danger of involvement. These were not the antisocial or asocial behaviors characteristic of the so-called psychopathic personality. Within the hospital several factors revealed compliant, conforming, and adaptive behavior. These may be termed defenses in that they serve to maintain distance—the good patient need not be given too much attention. Partially this was initiated by the staff's demand for adaptive behavior, but the fact that some could comply and others could not indicates that the capability for conforming and "as if" behavior was a salient characteristic of a type of borderline case.

The diagnosis *schizoid personality* is often applied to borderline patients. According to our current definitions, schizoids avoid close or competitive relations. However, they are shy and sensitive and indulge in considerable autistic thinking. Also, they rarely express open hostility or ordinary aggressive feelings. Finally, they may, and frequently do, develop overt schizophrenic psychoses.

Chapter 5
The Family of the
Borderline Patient

Research on the family has either of two major goals, depending on the orientation of the investigator. Those who search for influences of the family structure-function, expressed by internal disturbing forms of communication such as skew or the *double bind*, point toward the psychosocial etiology of various mental disorders including schizophrenia. More reductionistic researchers believe that family disturbances are markers indicating biogenetic origins of the schizophrenias. These opposing views reveal the dichotomous thinking of investigators, their either-or concepts, instead of the more sophisticated and modern philosophy of complementarity. There is no question that the methods of comparison between monozygotic and dizygotic twins, as well as study of the results of adoption of high-risk children by healthy parents, have increased our information about the biogenetic roots of the schizophrenias in the absence of any discovery of pathological genes.

However, disorders in the families of schizophrenic patients (Wender 1968) have been designated a *schizophrenic* spectrum, which we have criticized before as poorly defined. We are concerned that the spectrum of *chronic* schizophrenia includes acute schizophrenia as if it were a separate disease, schizoid character as if there were an acceptable universal definition, and borderline schizophrenia in terms not of the results of our statistical and actuarial data (Grinker and Werble 1968) but of Hoch and Polatin's *pseudoneurotic schizophrenias 1949)*. These last are not borderline cases in essence, but rather are real schizophrenias. For this reason we consider the inclusion of the borderline acute schizophrenia in the same spectrum as unfortunate, and in general think that the concept of schizophrenic spectrum constitutes circular reasoning.

Investigation of family patterns associated with mental disorders has advanced considerably over the past twenty years in a number of areas. The families of borderline patients, however, have received little attention or systematic study.* Psychodynamic theories of parent-child relations in the etiology of the borderline syndrome have been proposed by Masterson (1976) and Wolberg (1952).

Masterson presents an object-relations theory of the developmental origin of the borderline syndrome, based on his own clinical impressions and on the ideas of Kernberg (1967) and other psychoanalytically oriented clinicians (see chapter 2.) According to this view, the borderline patient suffers from a developmental arrest occurring at the separation-individuation phase in early childhood, an arrest caused by the mother's withdrawal of libidinal availability in reaction to the child's efforts to separate and individuate. The mother, usually seen as suffering a borderline syndrome herself, encourages the child's dependency in order to maintain her own emotional equilibrium. Threatened by and unable to deal with the child's emerging individuality, she discourages moves toward individuation by withdrawing support. The father is seen as playing a crucial negative instrumental role

*References to families of "borderline schizophrenics" (e.g. Wynne and Singer 1963) are not to be confused with the borderline syndrome.

in failing through either actual absence or emotional distance, to counteract this regressive pull, permitting the mother exclusive control of the child.

In Masterson's view, this process precipitates an abandonment depression in the child, who feels the mother's withdrawal at attempted individuation as a loss of part of himself. His later functioning and relationships become subordinate to defenses against feelings of abandonment, and he is particularly vulnerable to the stress of life events and developmental phases impinging upon the problem of separation and individuation. Clinical syndromes were found to be precipitated by events which challenged the capacity of the child for individuation or which threatened his clinging relationships to principal caretakers, especially loss through death or divorce.

From her clinical experience, Wolberg makes a number of generalizations about families of borderline cases. She states that borderline patients come from a disorganized family in which they lacked stable relations to any family member except perhaps an extended family member. The parents were unable to provide a functioning social unit. Mothers were found to be very disturbed in a variety of ways and were classified as (1) obsessive-compulsive; (2) narcissistic, competitive, and masculine; (3) paranoid; or (4) passive, schizoid. In Wolberg's view, the mother is there but really isn't; professes avid interest while deserting the child; goes through the role of homemaker and mother, performing all the "duties" of the role yet not giving thought to herself or the child as a person; and is preoccupied with her own fantasy world.

Wolberg describes four varieties of fathers of borderline patients: (1) passive-aggressive; (2) hostile, aggressive, attacking, and controlling; (3) paranoid; and (4) mildly psychopathic, promoting antisocial behavior.

From her observations, Wolberg proposes a model of triadic relations in the family of the borderline, based on Freud's continuum of acceptance/rejection in the severity of emotional disorders. Wolberg stresses the interaction between mother and father and posits different patterns for male and female offspring. For males, the father is rejecting of the son, *pushing him toward the mother.* The mother expresses hostility toward men by pitting son against father. Yet, because the son needs the father, he identifies with his hostile patterns, with ambivalence, guilt, and hatred. In the case of the female patient, the mother is seen as rejecting the daughter, *pushing her toward the father.* The father expresses hostility toward women by pitting daughter against mother. Thus, in Wolberg's view, the child develops identification fantasies serving as defense mechanisms against a traumatic family situation. These fantasies are thought to indicate the sadomasochistic role assigned the child by his parents when he becomes enmeshed as a scapegoat in the service of the parents defenses.

Neither Masterson nor Wolberg states the number of cases or characteristics of the samples from which these impressions were derived. Neither specifies study settings or methods, nor makes comparisons to other mental patients or to normals.

1968 Formulations

A limited investigation of the families of the borderline research patients was conducted by Grinker and Werble (1968) to describe the functioning of the family as a social system over time. Three important areas of functioning were dealt with:

1. How does the family function in relation to the patient's illness and hospitalization as a family crisis?
2. How does the family maintain the integration?
3. How does the family resist the natural process of disintegration?

The first question was answered by narrative statements taken from written records. A checklist of family traits was organized to measure the second and third questions. The major source of material was the standard social evaluation obtained routinely by social workers on the psychiatric unit. It included (1) assessment of family members and their views of the patient, illness, and hospitalization, and (2) background information, including the patient's development within his family and sociocultural context. Supporting data from psychiatric residents' summaries were also used. In all cases, informants included the patient and at least one family member.

A psychiatric social worker who had had no contact with the patients, the hospital unit, or other aspects of the study was trained to complete the checklists.* Each check, which represented the presence of a trait, was supported by a statement of evidence to insure its carefully considered factual basis.

SAMPLE CHARACTERISTICS

Of the fifty-one borderline research patients, information was available for forty-seven families of origin. Of the remaining four patients, two born illegitimately, two "had no families, and two families lived too far away for hospital contact."

At the hospital entry, over half (twenty-seven) of the single patients were living with their families of origin. Both parents were present in most homes, but in eleven cases one parent—usually the father—was absent. Thirteen patients currently had intact marriages; a few had marriages in the process of breaking up. Several separated, divorced, or single patients were living independently. Family heads were primarily in occupations classified as clerical, craftsman, operative, and service. A few were receiving public assistance.

FAMILY FUNCTIONING IN RELATION TO
THE PATIENT'S HOSPITALIZATION

The study question was described by three variables: (1) the family's involvement on behalf of the patient, e.g. keeping appointments, providing patient with needed articles, and

---

*The social worker and one author (B. W.) independently scored 15 patients not in the study and compared and discussed results.

planning for discharge; (2) the family's attitude toward hospitalization; and (3) the relevance of the patient's illness to the family.

Family involvement ranged from minimal or none to intense. Most frequently, some member—usually the patient's spouse or mother—cooperated with the unit social worker. Family attitude toward the patient's hospitalization varied, but was rarely indifferent. Yet only 36 percent perceived the fact of illness and the need for hospital care. Regarding etiology, half the families did not connect the illness to any contributing factor, and 32 percent attributed it to others or to external causes. A few, usually mothers, blamed themselves, indicating past behavior or inadequate child-rearing.

None of the measures was found to be associated with specific borderline subgroups. On the whole, the families of the borderline patients displayed a range of functioning in relation to their illness.

FAMILY INTEGRATION AND
RESISTANCE TO DISINTEGRATION

Three distinct family types were found by using a statistical clustering program. No one family type was found to be associated with a particular borderline subgroup.

Family type I: not a mutually protective unit: Nineteen families clustered on the presence of a set of traits describing the pathological way the family maintained its integration. In contrast to other families, this cluster was characterized by one trait, noted in all nineteen cases: "Family is not a mutually protective unit." Several other traits were consistent with this: discord, conflict, role-rejection, and confusion. These families also matched on the nonoccurrence of traits describing any resistance to the process of family disintegration, the very traits that characterized Type II families.

Family type II: excessively protective: Six families clustered on the presence of a set of traits that describe how the families resist the natural process of disintegration: "Family is excessively protective" was recorded for all families in this cluster. The chief traits describe a smothering, suffocating family. All six patients with Type II families were unattached males. On later follow-up none had married. The investigators considered this a testimonial to the resistance of these families to disintegration.

Family type III: denial of problems: Nine families were characterized by a denial of problems, absence of discordant marriages, and mixed parental affect with neither positive nor negative affect predominant.

In conclusion, the borderline patients came from three types of pathological families, differentiated from one another but unassociated significantly with the four patient subgroups. It should be noted that in one family cluster, five of the seven cases were female and were marked by (1) the trait of overattachment to the father, and (2) absence of the other traits studied.

FAMILIES OF PROCREATION

Data were analyzed for sixteen married patients who had children. Over half came from Type I families of origin. Not surprisingly, the traits characterizing the families of procreation most closely resembled the profile of Type I families of origin, "lacking a mutually protective unit and characterized by discord and conflict."

DISCUSSION

We urged caution in generalizing from this family study. The families were studied ex post facto, from preexisting records, and informants varied from family to family. Sample demographic characteristics were not specified, nor were control group comparisons made. Moreover, interview reports are limited by subjective bias, and family interaction was not directly assessed. Nevertheless, the data available were systematically rated and statistically analyzed. While etiological conclusions cannot be drawn from the data, there was no doubt that all the families studied were seriously disturbed.

Furthermore, the patients who married tended, as spouses and parents, to carry on the deviant behavior patterns reported for their families of origin.

Family Study 1976:
14 New Borderline Cases
By Froma Walsh, A.C.S.W.

In an attempt to shed more light on family patterns in the borderline syndrome, a limited retrospective study was conducted utilizing the fourteen borderline cases described in chapter 3. There are two aspects to the present report: (1) *summary family characteristics*, with attention to separation stresses and family relationship patterns as reported by all fourteen patients, and (2) a *family case illustration,* including interviews and projective data for mother, father, and patient and direct observation of family interaction.

SUBJECTS AND CONTEXT
Family data for the fourteen borderline cases were collected as part of a nonschizophrenic, hospitalized, mental patient control group in a comprehensive schizophrenia research program. Methods of selection and diagnosis of patients are outlined in chapter 3. The family study investigates family relational, structural, and communication patterns, employing interviews, questionnaires, projective techniques, and direct observation of family interaction, the latter limited to intact family triads (mother-father-child).

Extent of participation in the family study varies with the structure, availability, and consent of each family. This group of borderline cases had so few families intact (see findings, below) and so few parents available for direct study participation that it was decided to limit summary analysis of the borderline group to patient reports, which were available for all cases, and to present a case illustration where both parents were together and seen in all phases of the research.

METHODS

A. *Summary family characteristics:* To identify and summarize patterns occurring in patient reports of family relationships, two checklists were constructed, based on characteristics found by previous investigators in families of borderline patients.

1. *A list of separation stress events* was adapted from Masterson (1976), who observed that borderline patients were particularly vulnerable to change in life events which resulted in or threatened the loss of parental figures. Items were catagorized by (a) parents' marital changes, (b) child placement, (c) serious illness or death of parent or sibling, (d) subject attempt to leave home, and (e) attempt to establish a marriage and family.

An event was checked only when the patient's report gave clear evidence of its occurrence. The subject's age at the time of the event was recorded, as well as whether clinical symptoms appeared within a year of the event.

2. *Patient reports of family relationships* were recorded and then summarized on a checklist of descriptive phrases, including the relational attributes noted in the borderline studies of Grinker and Werble, Wolberg, and Masterson. Items were grouped in the following areas: (a) positive bond, (b) negative-conflictual, (c) overinvolved, (d) underinvolved, and (e) consistency-stability. Items were checked for each of the following relationships: (a) patient-mother, (b) patient-father, (c) mother-father, and (d) sibling-patient.

For an item to be checked, a direct statement by the patient was required. For instance, a check for the item "feels neglected by" required that the patient actually report that he "felt neglected by" a particular family member, or similar words. Statements requiring rater inference were not scored.

The source material included taped interviews, hospital admission interview summaries, and questionnaires. The rater,* who had no contact with this subject group, was

*Special acknowledgment to Linda Lewis, research assistant.

trained to score data in the manner of the Grinker-Werble study.

B. *Family case illustration:* A closer inspection of family patterns in one female borderline case utilized audio-taped interviews with mother, father, and patient and their twenty-minute interaction on a structured task requiring resolution of different opinions.

Standardized procedures were followed with the family. First, mother, father, and patient were separately asked to compose stories for a series of projective scenes selected for their usefulness in eliciting family relationship projections. Next, they were brought together and asked to compose a joint story for two scenes just done individually: first TAT card 2 and then MAPS, each triadic scene typically seen as a parent-child family unit interacting. The family was told only "to arrive at a joint story" in ten minutes, at which time the investigator would return and one member of the family would tell the story arrived at. As in the individual task, it was requested that the story have a beginning, middle, and end, and that the thoughts and feelings of characters be given. The joint task was observed through a one-way screen and audio-taped for later process and content analysis.

Finally, the family members returned to separate rooms for a post-task and interview. The post-task seeks perceptions of the family decision-making process just completed. The interview (1-2 hours) is semistructured to obtain (a) mother's, father's, and patient's perspectives on family life and relationships over the years, each from his unique position in the family; (b) recall of parents' families of origin, and (c) indications of empathic understanding of other family members from description of a recent interpersonal problem.

The taped data for this family were reviewed independently by the investigator and research assistant, and on comparison their impressions were very similar. While some judgments were involved in selecting and summarizing data, an attempt was made to limit inference and interpretation and to illustrate those themes and patterns which repeatedly occurred in statements and behavior.

FINDINGS

Subject characteristics and family demographic information for the borderline group are shown in Table 1. Nine
subjects were female; five were male. All fourteen were
Caucasian. Eight were Jewish, three Protestant, two Catholic,
and one was of mixed religious background. The father's
socioeconomic status was primarily middle class, ranging
from I-IV (Hollinshead-Redlich classification). In their sib-
ships, four subjects were middle children, three were the
youngest, and one was an only child.

Separation stresses: The most striking feature in this
borderline group is that only six of the fourteen patients came
from intact families. Eight patients suffered parent loss,
either through death (three cases, all fathers) or divorce (five
cases). One parent death was by suicide. Three of the five
children of divorced parents experienced further trauma in
parents' unstable remarriages or outright rejection by step-
parents.

To determine whether this high rate of parent loss was
specific to the borderline group, a comparison was made with
a group of eighty schizophrenic patients in the same study, of
comparable age, race, and socioeconomic status. The borderline group was found to have a significantly lower frequency
of intact families (42.9 percent) than the schizophrenics (73.8
percent), (Chi square = 5.33, sig. .025 level), as is shown in
Table 2.

Moreover, half the borderline cases had serious parent
illness—mental, physical, or both—requiring extended or
multiple hospitalization or with a chronic, deteriorating
course. Only three of the fourteen families did not have serious
parent illness or loss. Additionally, in four families a sibling
was seriously ill or died in infancy while the patient was
between the ages of one and six.

Thirteen borderline patients had reported the onset of major
symptoms within the year of attempted separation from
families. Most returned home. Suicide attempts occured in at
least five cases during shifts between home and away.

None of the male patients married, although one fathered a

Table 1. Borderline sample characteristics

Case	Type	Age	Sex	Marital Status	Religion	Socio-Economic Status	Parents' Marital Status	Sibship Size	Birth Order
6	I	24	F	S	J	III	F died, P: age 21	3	2
7	I	18	F	S	J	I	Divorced P:. age 9 Remarried P: age 12	3	1
8	I	24	M	S	C	III	Separated P: age 16; Divorced P: age 18; Remarried P: age 19	3	2
9	II	25	F	M	C	IV	Divorced; Remarried	3	2
10	II	29	M	S	J	III	F Died P: age 16		
11	II	20	F	S	P	III	Married	5	3
12	II	21	F	S	J	III	Married	2	1
13	III	19	M	S	J/C	III	Divorced P: age 5; F Remarried 3x; M Remarried P: age 8	3	1
14	III	22	M	S	J	II	Married	2	2
15	III	26	F	Sep	P	IV	Born illegitimate F unknown M married 5x	3	3
16	III	19	M	S	J	II	Married	3	1
17	IV	22	F	S	J	II	Married	3	1
18	IV	28	F	D	P	II-III	F. Died P: age 11	1	1
19	IV	19	F	S	J	II	Married	3	3

**Table 2. Percentage of intact families of origin
for borderline and schizophrenic patients**

Family of Origin	Borderline		Schizophrenic	
Intact biological	6	42.9%*	59	73.8%*
Divorce	5	35.7%	12	15.0%
Parent death	3	21.4%	7	8.8%
Adoption	0	0 %	2	2.5%

* x^2 =5.33
  Sig.   = .025

child and then abandoned the mother and child. Of three
female patients who married, all had serious problems, two
ending in divorce.

It should be noted that in the seven cases in which the dates
of grandparents' deaths were known, four occurred in the year
of onset of illness, two occurred in the year of the patient's
birth, and one family lost all four grandparents in World War
II. The data also reveal that a number of parents themselves
experienced separation trauma in childhood. The background
of the father in one intact family of a female borderline patient
(Case 11) is a case in point:

> At age three, he was placed in a foster family when his parents
> divorced and his father went to prison for twenty years. When he
> was seven, his mother remarried but did not take him back. At
> age ten, he spent a year in a hospital with rheumatic fever. At
> eleven, because he was homeless, he was admitted in a state
> school for boys, an inappropriate placement, as it was chiefly for
> delinquents. At fourteen, he was taken to live with his mother,
> stepfather, and three stepsibs. But within a year he was expelled
> from the home because the family dog was run over while he was
> walking it. A stepsister reported, "Jim killed the dog," and the
> stepfather replied, "Get rid of him."

Summary characteristics of family relationships: The relationships between parents and child as described by the patients were most notably characterized by *underinvolvement.* Twelve of the fourteen patients described the relationships with one or both parents as distant and lacking in feelings of relatedness, with parents described as "remote," "aloof," "detached," and "preoccupied." It is of note that all nine women used such adjectives. Half of the patients (two males, five females) stated they felt neglected by a parent, in all cases except for one of the males, by the mother.

Instability has been noted by other authors as a characteristic of families of borderlines. Our finding of the high rate of broken homes has been noted above. In these families, four of the patients described the remaining parent, usually the mother, as "unreliable," "undependable," and "erratic" in moods and behavior. Also, in four cases of parent divorce, patients reported a conflict of loyalty to parents whose hatred of each other persisted after divorce, so that the child was threatened with rejection by one parent should he or she get close to the other.

Nine patients (five males and four females) described a strong negative or conflictual relationship with parents, characterized by hostility or open rejection by their parents, contemptuous or belittling attitudes of parents toward them, or frank physical or sexual abuse. Three of the five males felt their parents to be overly critical and demeaning of them and felt themselves to be a disappointment to their parents— especially to their fathers.

Eight patients (two males and six females) felt "overinvolved with" or "special to" a parent, yet they specified that this was in the sense of being made overdependent on their parents. They felt controlled by their parents and obligated to comply with parental needs and expectations—primarily in the service of the parents—in a manner rigid, unrealistic, and hardly in keeping with their own needs and abilities. In every case where a "special" relationship was mentioned, the patient felt that, underneath, he was not genuinely cared about or understood by the parent and that his own needs and feelings were ignored.

The marital unit was reported to be conflictual, with rejection or demeaning attitudes between spouses in eleven cases. Two of the six intact marriages were also characterized as overdependent. *Sibling relations* were reported to be highly conflictual in eleven of thirteen cases where there were siblings. Patients tended to feel inferior to siblings and felt siblings to be hostile, rejecting, or uncaring toward them. Five patients felt no emotional bond to any of their siblings. Yet in three other cases the patient's only affective bond in the family had been with an older nurturant sibling no longer available.

In summary, these limited patient reports suggest family patterns of unrelatedness, neglect, rejection, and disappointment by one or both parents. It is significant that a poor or nonexistent relationship with one parent was not offset by a genuinely positive one with the other, or rarely even with siblings. Thus, the parental unit failed to provide basic nurturance, protection, or empathic caring. In none of the fourteen cases did the child feel that either parent understood his needs or feelings. Following are the data obtained from the family interviews and interaction for one case.

FAMILY CASE ILLUSTRATION:
THE A. FAMILY (CASE 17 OF CHAPTER 3)

The A. family is an upper middle-class suburban Jewish family. Mr. A. is a self-made businessman, with a high school education. Mrs. A. works full-time with her husband. The patient is the eldest daughter in a sibship of three girls, each two years apart.

The patterns they describe in their family relations, particularly in the parental unit, the sibship, and the patient's roles and relationships, suggest the presence of a number of the problems seen in the borderline group above.

Parental unit: Overdependency has characterized the parents' marital relationship over the years. Mr. A. states of his wife, "She spends no time away from me. We get up in the morning together, drive to work together, go out for lunch together, have dinner together, and clean up together." While this is portrayed as his wife's need, it also serves his acknowledged need to have others rely on him. He adds, noting his longstanding discomfort in social situations, "It's more comfortable than seeking companions."

Mrs. A., a compulsively hard worker, has severe anxiety which prevents her independent functioning. For instance, she is unable to drive because she is always nervous and expects the worst to happen. She describes how "once a year I blow my top and say I'm leaving and I pack my bag but I only get as far as the car; then I remember that I can't drive."

The parents' dependent relationship is regarded by the patient as "sick." "My mom has to be with him all the time or she gets hysterical. He used to go on business trips but stopped because she'd get too upset. *She was too dependent so I decided I couldn't be like that. I have to be independent and strong.*"

Sibship: The three daughters reportedly *fought constantly* while growing up. The father states, "The only problems my wife and I ever have are over the children. Children are always problems to parents. The girls created problems for us all the time. But they're basically good children—at leat I'd like to think they are." The patient felt that the fights helped her mother "get out her insecurities. She'd always get into it and tell us how horrible children are." The middle sibling was always regarded as "the problem child," and was taken to psychiatrists from the age of six.

While growing up, the two younger sisters tended to gang up on the patient. She wanted a closed relationship with them, but they always *excluded* her. The patient states, "*I never felt they cared about me* one way or the other." The father notes, "There was no great feeling of affection between them."

Both parents remark that each of their daughters has complained of being *neglected and less loved* by the parents than were the others. The father notes, "Each one has actually said they felt like a stepchild in this family." It is of interest that the father, throughout his interview, only once referred to a daughter by name, instead referring to them as "the oldest one," "the middle one," and "the youngest one."

Patient roles and relationships with parents: The mother described the patient as "very sweet, very kind, *exceptionally good,* and very understanding." The patient saw her own role in the family as "the good child," the one who would "stop fights, never get emotional, never cry" because her parents expected her to be good. She always felt they had *higher expectations* of her than of the others: "to be good, to work hard, to achieve in school, and to be grateful for an education." The latter she saw as her father's expectation, to make up for his own inability to attend college due to financial pressures.

The patient *never felt emotionally close to either parent.* Both parents were preoccupied with their needs and her fulfillment of them. She was special to her father, in his intellectual and academic expectations of her. Yet she regretted that their contact was limited to abstract political discussion (about "the needs of the masses"), with never any expression of their own personal feelings. Also, she felt pressured to perform academically beyond her only average abilities in order to gain his interest and approval. She felt she had disappointed him with her school failure. Moreover, she felt her special position with her father was a source of jealousy and resentment for her sisters.

The patient saw herself as listener to all her mother's complaints. She noted with resentment that her mother "keeps her friends by listening to their problems—but never to mine. When it comes to talking or when I had a problem, when I was younger, she couldn't talk or help out. Say if I had feelings about something, I'd get the message from her: 'Don't! Really, no, go away!' So I just made them go away and I was very strong and kept my feelings inside. Except I got terrible headaches. Later by taking pills I had no awareness of my feelings."

When asked how that pattern came about, the patient replied that her mother and father were "just *unable to deal with emotions,* each in a different way. *Mother gets frustrated and cries but she doesn't know what she's crying about.* She's had emotional breakdowns, but no treatment." In contrast, "Father always acted strong and reserved. When I was upset he used to take me to work with him rather than talk about why I was crying. I had to do extreme things—get hysterical or take pills to make him know there's something wrong. *He's all intellect—no feelings.* Now in the hospital he brings me books for my mind, to keep my intellect intact."

The patient adds, *"If I'm sick, like now, they'll take care of me, but if I'm well I have to take care of my mother, her emotional needs.* It's always been that way; it's been a major responsibility. Except when I'm sick—then they give me an aspirin and take me to a doctor." Thus, caretaking roles are generationally reversed, and even when the patient is ill, parental response lacks nurturance.

Family unit: There was little shared interest or activity as a family. The father recalls, "We didn't spend time together properly. I was always working very hard, very busy, and didn't have the patience for them. I came home at night and didn't want to be bothered with children. We always tried to eat together, but after that, that was the end of the family. We never played with them or took them for activities or vacations together."

The parents also noted that decision making and discipline were "never uniform—always inconsistent." The father states, "My wife would say one thing, I would say another, or one of us would lose our temper, yell at them, or smack them. They learned quickly who to go to for what, who would *concede.* They learned how to play us off. We should have had a united front *against* them." Mother, too, views the process in terms of battle and concession, with one side (parents) *giving in* to the other (children).

Separation concerns appear prominent in the family. In the past four years, three grandparents have dies and all three daughters have left home. The onset and exacerbation of the patient's syndrome occurred at such times, and she returned home. The mother reported a panic attack last year that began while taking the youngest daughter—and the last at home— away to college. The mother felt on the verge of a nervous breakdown and for three months couldn't leave the house or go anywhere alone. It subsided around the time the patient returned home and then recurred just after the patient's hospitalization. It would appear that the mother has difficulty coping when the patient is not available to fill a parentified caretaking role.

Finally, there is a quality pervading the parental style of living up to some stereotyped expectations about what parents and families "should" do, yet a profound sense of having failed to give emotionally, or to understand one another. The father states that his wife "has always done all the things you would think are important, that are good, that you would expect a mother to do, such as PTA and scout leader, *yet I don't think she understood her children.*" Yet the father feels he failed even to be involved. Despite his hight academic expectations of the girls, "I only went to the school when I had to." Still, he concludes, "We tried to give them the *impression* of closeness and affection and care and concern for each other and for them."

The mother concludes in her interview, *"He (Mr. A.) is not the kind you can sit down and talk to; he can't give of himself or listen to the other."* Yet, she adds, "He loves his children; he's by far the best of us. I'm always the worrier—I always see the worst. . . .I have a lot of feeling, but when I want to express it, it never comes out right: it is lost somewhere. . . .I wanted children but not everyone is made to be a mother. I don't believe I should have had children. I wasn't cut out for it. . . .I gave all the things I was supposed to but I guess there was just something in myself they needed that I didn't give. Each child says 'You loved this one better than me.' A very unhappy home with the children."

The roots of these family patterns can be seen in the families of origin.

Families of origin: Mrs. A., the youngest child in a sibship of five, conveyed no sense of relatedness to her parents. She gave a detailed, impersonal description of them as hard workers, each preoccupied with more important activities outside the home. Mrs. A's mother, "an unusual woman," a nurse and community worker, had been one of eighteen children in her family of origin.

Mr. A. was the middle child in a sibship of five boys, the first

four born within five years. When in his interview he
described family relations, he never reported his own feelings
but rather replied impersonally, in terms of the sibship en
bloc: "All good sons—helped the parents and helped each
other out."

There was little nurturance or interest on the part of his
parents. Mr. A. recalls his father as strict and stern,
preoccupied with a number of illnesses over the years. His
parents were not happy together. "My father was a meek,
quiet little man with not much to say; my mother thought he
had no backbone." The family "got along quietly—sat around
reading with not much to say. They were not hard to get along
with; neither one had strong opinions and they didn't expect
much from the children. There was little affection. Hugging
and kissing were never done. I don't remember ever kissing
my mother as a young boy; *of course we were never leaving.*"

In fact, Mr. A continued living at home until he married at
age twenty-six. "If I hadn't married, I still would be living at
home. It never would have occurred to me to go out and live
someplace else."

The brothers took financial care of their parents until their
recent deaths, which occurred just prior to the patient's onset
of illness and hospitalization. In light of the father's
dependency-separation problems, it is clear that the patient
assumed a caretaking role toward him as well as toward his
mother.

Parent loss and caretaking issues go back at least another
generation. Mr. A's father lost his mother in his early teens,
"overcoming the loss by becoming a hardworking man like
his father." When Mr. A.'s mother was a small child, her
mother died and her father remarried, not taking her with
him. "She was passed from cousin to cousin, aunt to aunt. She
never knew either parent."

Postinterview task: Interview reports of family relations
were supported by postinterview task presentations. When
asked to describe a recent interpersonal problem in the family,
the father's response was as follows. First, he was unable to

think of any problem. Next, he recalled having an argument with his wife but could not remember what it was about, so he decided to describe a problem with the patient. He gave a lengthy circumstantial account, but failed to demonstrate any capacity to understand or experience her behavior in terms of feelings or authentic motives. He showed a limited ability for empathy and a failure to integrate feelings and experience of self and others in his cognitive framework.

Family interaction: The interaction of this family was characterized by a striking inability to share in the different perceptions of each family member or to collaborate as a family unit on any joint task. Each individual presented and held adamantly to his own view, failing repeatedly to acknowledge that another's view, although different, might be equally valid or even of interest. The means of resolving differences was to "concede" or "give in" to another, rather than to compromise or synthesize. Below are the family's comments on this process as they argued over which of the three separate stories to present:

Mother: You know I'm the bossy type. I think I'm right! (laughs)
Father: I like my story better.

Mother: We'll never get together on this story, I can see that. We have none of us convinced each other.

Mother: We'll have to beat each other down. (laughs)

Mother: We all don't agree; how can we come—what can we say? That means that just one of us would have to tell their story because not one of us will *give in* that we see the story the other way, right?

On both task stories, the family failed to agree on one joint story, even after requesting and taking several minutes longer than the allotted time. When the same impasses occurred on the second task, the family as a group attempted resolution by repeating the same pattern, each with a new story. On the first task, the mother finally capitulated to her husband: "I'll agree with anything you say."

Thus, decisions were made without regard to the feelings of family members or the merits of ideas, but rather on the basis of concession. The mother's weakening position and dependence on the father for her structuring were seen in the second task. When the father introduced his story, the mother immediately doubted the validity of her perception (M: Boy, I was way off on that one) when, actually, hers was a story more typically given than the father's. After the mother related her story, the father failed to acknowledge it with any comment, shifting discussion back to his own story. Later, he failed to recall the mother's story at all.

The daughter was largely excluded from the transactional process. Her opinions and feelings were rarely sought and when spontaneously expressed were ignored. She was shut out of the parental alliance achieved by the mother's yielding her own position to support the father.

A pattern of parental lack of interest in others, separateness, and self-preoccupation pervaded the thematic content of the family's stories as well as the process, as on TAT card 2:

Father: I think it's a very nice picture. It's a nice family arrangement.
Mother: I don't think so, I think the three of them look rather disinterested in each other. Each one is separate, each one is thinking about what they're doing. And they each have their own...
Father: Well, each one isn't certainly, each one is an individual who is involved...
Mother: ...with himself.

Mother: Look at the mother's face. She doesn't look like she's interested in anything. She's got a faraway look. She doesn't look like she's uh...

Daughter: . . . interested in her daughter.
Mother: Interested in either one. She looks like she's uh. . .
Daughter: Right on.
Mother: . . . just dreaming.

Mother: And it looks like the father is very interested in his work. All right? We all know that. And, uh, the mother, really, she's not looking at her daughter in any way. She's got her eyes half closed and she's thinking about herself. . . . She's really, nothing is bothering her too much.

Family members also exluded parent or child characters from their stories. The patient saw no father figure at all on card 2:

D: And that's her brother, by the way, They have no father.
F: Well, I thought that was her father.
M: (softly) That's what I thought.

Mother and father then joined in attempting to present a "nice" image, he focusing on superficial appearances and she denying neglect or anything "bad."

M: That's a very nice farm, well taken care of.
F: Well, the fields are plowed straight on it.
M: I mean there's no—no neglect or anything, so nothing bad. . . . It looks like . . .
F: Right.
M: . . . nothing bad happened there.
F: Well, I think they're well dressed.

A circular pattern occurred. As the daughter was ignored, her interruptions increased and her remarks and tone became increasingly negative, sarcastic, and sharp. Yet the more negative she became, the more her ideas and feelings were ignored, minimized, or countered. Struggle ensued between father and daughter, with the mother entering to support the father's press for a "nice" story:

F: Which story shall we present?
D: Mine.
F: Why? Is yours the nicest story?
D: No. It's not supposed to be a nice story.
F: Why not? Shouldn't stories be nice stories?
M: Well, I think it is nice because you said that there's....
D: Why *should* stories be nice?
F: What's wrong with a nice story? I like stories that always hap...end happily.
D: All stories don't end happily.

The struggle ended in deadlock and the father shifted focus.

The central concerns and problems in this family were further revealed in process and story content on the second joint storytelling task for the MAPS scene. The mother's story again showed her frustration with an uninterested father who wouldn't respond, and represented her separation concerns as a parental inability to "control" a child, that is, to keep him from leaving home:

M: (Identifies the three figures as mother, father, and son) And the father is rather disinterested, like he never took an interest....what can he do? The son says "I'm leaving whether you like it or not!" and that's it. And the father stays like a...he just, he never has anything to say. He isn't going to say anything anyway. The mother...neither of them can control him anyway. He's going.

The father added, suggesting his own unresolved separation concerns:

F: The son was going to *escape*, uh, leave home.

Next, in the father's story, a child figure was not seen. A story was told about a couple who want to buy a nice house from a salesman. The patient interrupted to ask:

D: Do they have children?
F: Where's the money going to come from?

D: Do they have children?
M: (to F) Boy, I'm all for your story.
F: (to M) I didn't hear you. Hmm?
M: (laughs)
D: Do they have children?
F: *No*, they have no children yet. (F continues his account)

The patient's own story, told last, is of interest, considering her long history of migraine headaches and the concerns expressed later in her interview:

D: My story was very different. It's a wife, husband, and brother-in-law. He brought his brother home for dinner. She'd been cleaning house all day but he didn't tell her what time. And the woman gets headaches, bad headaches, which she's having now. And she didn't finish making dinner. And he's telling her, "Get into the kitchen and make dinner." And, uh, she goes and makes dinner and excuses herself during dinner with her bad headache. And um, yet she doesn't say anything to him. She never says anything to him. She never tells him how she feels. And the brother-in-law... after she left, he tells his brother that maybe these headaches she keeps getting are from something about the way she feels. And that maybe he's a little hard on her. And he goes upstairs later on, the husband, has a talk with his wife and says he will try to be more understanding, and do the best he can. And, not knowing what she feels ever, 'cause she's so confused all the time, she doesn't even know what her feelings are. She, um, says, "All right now. Just kind of try it again." And that's the end of my story.
F: Well, which story do we like the best? (Shifting focus)
D: You don't like it 'cause I said the father's disinterested and the mother gets headaches?
F: (sharply) You want to change the story? I'll give you... I'll, I'll give you a new story if you want to make it more sordid!

When pressed to acknowledge the daughter's story, the father labeled her problem theme as "sordid" and countered it with an outrageous story. His indirect message warns: "If you insist that I see a problem I'll give you a much worse problem that will upset you!" In the process of this labeling and threat, the initial problem presented was minimized and dismissed. There was no further reference to the daughter's story as the parents considered new possibilities. When the investigator returned, the father informed him:

F: My wife prefers that the family is breaking up as a group and this one (referring to his daughter) prefers tha. . . .that, you know, they're having all kinds of major problems. I like ha. . .stories with happy endings.

Interestingly, the mother then appointed the daughter to tell her story, indirectly suggesting that her daughter, and possibly her symptoms, might also speak for the mother. Yet afterward, when the investigator asked if the story were agreeable to the others, the parents closed with:

M: No, but that's okay.
F: No, I . . . I would like, like I say, I like happy stories. And I . . . I don't see all that in that picture.

In summary, the family interaction process and story thema were characterized by a lack of empathic relatedness. There was a noticeable lack of (1) statements of confirmation of others' viewpoints, (2) investigatory questions aimed at understanding why or how another's views were held, and (3) statements showing sensitivity, interest, or care as regards the other family members, their ideas, or feelings. Members, locked in separate positions and unable to compromise or synthesize, struggled for control, finally resolving the struggle only through concession. Throughout, the patient was largely ignored by the parents, with the mother accommodating the father.

The projective stories were notable for the absence of father or child characters, and for the isolation, separateness, lack of interest, and self-preoccupation of family members, especially parental figures. Separation concerns were also evident. The parents, especially the father, showed a strong investment in avoidance and denial of problems, and in presentation of "nice" impressions and "happy" stories.

In short, the family's transactional process and their projective theme tend to support later interview reports of family life by mother, father, and patient alike.

FAMILY STUDY COMMENTS

In studying the families of the fourteen borderline cases, the sample size and available data limited our aims and methods to descriptive patient reports of family characteristics. Our intention was to identify and summarize common relationship patterns, recognizing that there was both overlap and variability within the group. The number of males was too small to note any gender-related trends. Time limitations did not allow control group comparisons beyond the variable of family intactness. The case illustration was intended as a fuller impression of patterns in one family, combining perspectives of mother, father, and patient with direct observation of their interaction.

In general, our findings were consistent with the impressions of earlier investigators. Hopefully, our study will contribute to the identification of critical family variables for more systematic study.

Our major finding was the high frequency of parent loss for the borderline patients. Reports of patients from intact families, and in particular the family case illustration, suggest that even when both parents are in the home they both fail to relate empathically to the needs and feelings of each other and of the child.

Chapter 6
Psychological Case Studies

Dr. Doris Gruenewald, with the help of Dr. Mary Rootes, studied with psychological methods some of our original borderline patients. Our own methods in the original study were restricted to observations and descriptions of behavior on the nursing unit of a psychiatric hospital (Illinois State Psychiatric Institute), where experienced psychologists with sufficient expertise were at the time unavailable. Drs. Gruenewald and Rootes presented their research procedure in the following memorandum.

"We see the purpose of our phase of the overall borderline study as being to obtain a picture of the mental interior (the semiprivate perceptions, thoughts, fantasies, etc.) of the group of subjects whose ego-functioning, as evidenced in more public behaviors, has already been extensively sampled. The information we obtain may assist in diagnosing borderline ego-functioning in cases where behavioral data is much less reliable and extensive than that made available under the special conditions of the investigation reported by the Grinker group.

"Our conceptions regarding the fruitful use of clinical test data lead us to expect that evidence bearing on personality constructs of the kind Grinker, Werble, and Drye use to characterize the borderline syndrome (self-image, self-esteem, pervasive hostility, etc.) will appear most clearly when our data are integrated across tests rather than across persons. We believe there is no reason to anticipate that single test scores will be substantially differentiating. Our general hypothesis is that the attitudes toward self and toward others revealed in a variety of ways throughout the test protocols will be distinguishable from those of other clinical groups in terms of such characteristics as stability, organization, affective quality, and conformity to social norms. Accordingly we plan to use a full clinical battery of tests, (WAIS, Rorschach, House-Tree-Person,TAT, with possible additions as individual cases may require) and employ the usual contextual and internal consistency checks of the case-study approach as our chief guarantors of objectivity. We feel this far from ideal course preferable to the pseudoobjectivity of computing averages of discrete test scores, where the scores are, in themselves, relatively meaningless.

"On an experimental basis, we would like to include three objectively scorable personality tests that provide a set of ratios or some other device designed to integrate 'globally' the subject's pattern of response to the test. Although yielding only a dichotomous classification, Meehl's set of four score comparisons for the MMPI appears promising for the differentiation of psychotics from neurotics. Providing a fuller classificatory scheme, Loevinger's Scale of Ego Development permits assignment of subjects to one of six ego levels ranging from 'impulse-ridden' to 'autonomous.' Rootes's Activity Scale provides for *shaky* assignment to one of four groups presumed to vary in maturity of self-evaluation response (based on the evidences of discrimination and balance in the pattern of test responses). While none of these global scores approach the comprehensiveness of scope that would be desirable for ego assessment, they provide for *some* within-subject integration of data. Their potential merit as research tools lies in their objective and relatively rapid scoring and greater freedom from the bias inherent in examiner-subject interaction. In our study these tests may, if time limits necessitate it, be completed by the subject at home and mailed to us. Since there is no evidence at this point that these scores have validity for differentiating borderline subjects from neurotic or psychotic, we include them primarily for the help these subjects may give us toward understanding the test scores, rather than vice versa. In order that our psychological case studies may provide an additonal independent check on the validity of these instruments, we plan to put these tests aside and look at them only after the case studies are completed."

Vignettes of Patients
Used for Psychological Studies

R.C., a patient presented in the appendix of our original study, was a *vigorous and boisterous female* with an IQ of 115, a broad cultural background, verbal superiority, and good psychomotor control. *She had a sense of helplessness and inadequacy, giving up easily and calling for help.* She was excessively anxious to succeed. *She behaved in a restricted manner and had limited interaction with other people, with whom she demonstrated an "as if" quality, acting appropriately in an effort to please but avoiding genuine interpersonal involvement.* Her satisfactions rested on daydreams which included *hostility.* Her focal conflict was in the heterosexual field; being baited by men left her feeling destroyed. "I am always put upon and taken advantage of and there is no alternative to this relationship." *She settles for an empty, drab existence in defense against being rejected, thereby losing sight of boundaries between the aggressor and the victim. She does not, however, become psychotic. (Group I)*

J.K., with an IQ of 104 and a comprehensive vocabulary, is strictly religious, with self-abnegation but angry and paranoid over trivialities. His thirteen responses are brief and he retreats to *a waiting posture without hope*. Depression often breaks through when confronted by his unacceptable homosexual impulses. He neglects his body and has no teeth or dentures. (Group III)

M.M. is bland, empty, and dependent but not overtly depressed. Although she understands (IQ 102) *she cannot carry through social demands*. Everything is rosy on the surface as she follows external guidelines in the direction of thought disorder. *She has a poor sense of identity.* (Group III)

L.S. *has early disturbed object relations, going toward and away from people* like a yo-yo. She knows many people but has no friends. (Group II)

W.W. complies with expectations, about which fact he is "hung up." *He has no real relations*: only with prostitutes. His though processes are undisturbed but when abstaining from alcohol he becomes depressed. (Group III)

P.S. *has blurred reality contact, with affect storms leading to transient psychotic episodes.* He solves problems erratically, ending in *anger*. There is awareness but no insight. He has learned to live with these traits, behaving in a guarded fashion. (Group I)

W.S. *is a dependent person solving problems erratically* and frequently becoming *angry* at *frustrated dependency.* (Group IV)

F.B. has had a marginal adjustment as a homosexual. He stopped drinking by going to A.A. and stopped drugs. *He is aware of a difficulty in dealing with people but nevertheless has tremendous rage attacks following which he withdraws into fantasy.* There is no severe cognitive disturbance and he has learned to control himself and avoid panic. He is severely dependent on his mother and her family. He has some obsessive qualities. (Group II)

L.S. is phobic, staying in her apartment so that people can make no demands on her. Her IQ is 116 and her social comprehension excellent, but she has difficulty in performance, being interested only in surface qualities. *She is dependent, inadequate, and leans on a sick role* (hypochondriasis). (Group III)

D. B. has a verbal IQ of 113 and a performance IQ of 88 but is constricted, restricted, and depressed. *He is isolated, living alone and feeling lonely, with no anticipation of any future. He cannot invest in his environment. He is hopeless, defeated, and angry.* There are no schizophrenic thought disorders and alcohol is used as a defense. (Group IV)

The Gruenewald Report*

It is to be expected that no two assessment methods tap exactly the same aspects and levels of functioning. Nevertheless, the raw data of the borderline syndrome research and of this study have in common a representation of time-limited behavior segments whose analysis rests on an ego-psychological theoretical base. From each set of data structural, dynamic, and genetic components may be extrapolated. The conclusions drawn from a combined analysis of test protocols, observed behavior, and quality of interpersonal relatedness to the examiner necessarily differ in some respects from those of the original investigators. However, on the whole there is good agreement with previous findings, and in no case is the diagnosis of borderline unequivocally counterindicated.

Clearly the borderline category encompasses a variety of personality types and aspects of psychopathology which in varying degree are found in other nosological classifications. *Solely on the basis of test records,* two of the subjects could

*Reprinted by permission of the author and the American Medical Association (copyright, 1970) *Archives of General Psychiatry* 23:180-184, 1970

have been diagnosed schizophrenic: one paranoid, the other chronic undifferentiated, both in remission. In another case, depression was prominent enough to warrant a diagnosis of chronic depressive reaction. One of the cases might have been designated a passive-aggressive personality, passive-dependent type, and two looked like primitive hysterical characters. Lastly, the protocol of one subject might have been evaluated psychopathic. It was in the process of integrating test protocols with overall activity and life patterns that *borderline emerged as the primary diagnosis.*

The subjects are neither overtly psychotic nor exclusively neurotic. Maladaptive primary process manifestations are present in some but not all protocols in terms of content as well as formal thought organization. Basic patterns and intellectual capacity determine the degree and mode in which pathology is expressed. Defensive operations lie on a continuum from well-entrenched firmness to shaky lability. They range from obsessional, intellectualized dwelling on threatening inner issues to bland, affectless denial that such issues exit; from overideational exhaustion of details to repressive constriction of perceptual-cognitive functioning; and from paranoid projection and rejection of personal responsibility to overcompensatory, unrealistic conviction of competence. Depression is with a few exceptions not admitted to conscious experience but is in various forms indirectly expressed in most of the projective test protocols. All subjects, but especially those of potentially superior intelligence, function below their intellectual capacity. Some use their linguistic ability to bolster their low self-esteem and to achieve fantasy gratification. Others use words to cover up their inner emptiness or to relieve hostile feelings.

All show evidence of problems in handling of impulses, whether in terms of rigid overcontrol or labile, undifferentiated undercontrol. The means whereby each individual deals with his drives and impulses depend on his basic personality and vary according to factors inherent in his total field situation.

As for the adequacy of ego organization within each personality type, test results obtained six to eight years after

hospitalization indicate more or less arrested ego development and loosely defined ego boundaries with varying degrees
of fusion of normally discrete functions. Related to this
finding are signs of early disturbances in object relations,
pointing to a common etiological factor and lending weight to
a genetic and structural theoretical position vis-a-vis the
borderline syndrome.

The last of the questions posed at the outset concerns the
degree of congruence of past with present functioning and
movement across subgroups. In eight of the ten cases the
records fit the characteristics of the subgroup to which each
subject was assigned. Three excerpts of the clinical work-ups
will suffice to illustrate similarities and differences. The first
case represents agreement in both studies on group II
placement. The second case, formerly assigned to group III, is
now seen as belonging to group II. The third case is a typical
instance of the group III personality.

CASE EXAMPLES:

Case 1: There is nothing striking in the neat and conventional appearance of this thirty-two-year-old man. His major
mode of functioning is summed up in his manner of
responding to the invitation to participate in the follow-up
studies. He filled out the questionnaire mailed to him volubly
and frankly, writing of himself in the third person, but did not
contact the clinic as requested. He eagerly agreed to come in
when we called him on the phone, and appeared punctually at
the appointed hour. He started speaking the moment he was
met in the waiting room and did not stop until the end of the
three-hour interview.

He is keenly observant of himself and sensitively tuned in to
interpersonal transactions, albeit in a highly egocentric
fashion. He uses others' reactions as a check on his own
mental activity and has learned to use self-awareness
constructively for reality testing and control over affect and
thought content. His intellectual capacity is superior but not
functionally available for creating a life commensurate with
his abilities. However, he maintains a significant separation
between appropriate and inappropriate behavior in a given

situation and uses his relatively integrated intellectual resources in a highly circumstantial, obsessional manner for control over drives and affect. There is a continuous struggle between the more mature and the infantile, archaic ego in which the former frequently loses out. Fantasy activity, though prominent, does not flow into hierarchical organization but reflects a prevailing fragmentation of ego-functions. There is no firm boundary between inside and outside. Withdrawal into fantasy, aimed at reconstituting viable self- and object-representations, actually results in a further *splitting of objects* whose threatening, malevolent aspects then become even more emphasized.

At the root of this process are frankly oral-dependency needs persisting in infantile form, not assimilated into the developing ego and therefore beyond genuine ego control. The fluidity of internal boundaries permits these needs and their derivatives to blanket all aspects of the personality. Emotional balance in always in jeopardy. *Object hunger and object fear* continue to dominate and determine overt behavior, and a more than marginal adjustment cannot be expected.

In another case, originally assigned to group III, present functioning is at variance with the characteristics of that group. The subject is now considered to belong to group II. Assuming that group membership reflects an enduring personality organization within which fluctuations from more to less overt pathology, and vice versa, can occur, it would seem that this subject's earlier group placement was in error. On the other hand, he displayed a good deal of behavior then and now that could be considered evidence of group III characteristics. The "as if" quality is noted in the following sentence taken from the clinical interpretation of the test protocal: "He seems to know what the world looks like to others and he tries to conform to this knowledge without being able to bring it off." The fact that his total protocol contradicts group III membership draws attention to the advisability of using psychological tests in the process of full evaluation. Behavior alone may be a common final pathway for a number of underlying factors, and perusal of this patient's hospital record tends to support the opinion that some of these were overlooked.

Case 2: This thirty-year-old, unremarkable-looking man was initially guarded and reluctant to communicate. He loosened up when he was reassured that the interview was not specific to him and the condition for which he was hospitalized, but was part of a larger project.

He presented as severely and chronically depressed, with the classical sequence of anger/guilt/self-recrimination/self-punishment. His intellectual capacity is above average and potentially superior. However, he is handicapped in that the depressive process lowers his efficiency and prevents investment of sufficient energy to overcome obstacles. His level of anxiety is high and further interferes with his attention span and capacity for concentration.

Little is available to him in terms of fantasy resources, and integration of internalized imagery with external perception is impoverished. Object- and self-representations are under the shadow of negative affect which distorts all his relationships. He seems continually to feel under attack for what he conceives himself to be—a loathsome creature. But he also feels frustrated in his need for care and nurturance and on that level senses a grandiose, narcissistic innocence. There is a cry for help in spite of his basic hopelessness, yet he defeats therapeutic assistance through his *inability for genuine involvement.*

Case 3: This twenty-eight-year-old man looks younger than his stated age. There is something of the "dead-end kid" about him. His facial expression is bland. Though he laughs occasionally, he presents himself as even-tempered. He is at once subservient, arrogant, and covertly derogatory.

In the interview, he was constantly alert to cues from the examiner to guide his attitudes and behavior. He spoke of the desirability of further schooling to obtain a college degree which would enable him to have a white-collar or professional job instead of the manual labor he now performs, but he also was at pains to differentiate between education and intelligence. He emphasized his intellectual capacity and artistic talent, both of which are less than he likes to believe, and he projected his inability to implement his fantasies on external factors. He minimized a record of juvenile delinquency and berated the army psychiatrist who rejected him as unfit for military service, and he suspected that the present interview was for the purpose of checking up on him.

He was relectant to engage himself in the tests for fear of exposing deficiencies he was partly aware of. His intelligence level is slightly above average, but his use of high-flown expressions, often incorrect, is designed to make himself appear intellectual. The record indicates little capacity for empathic identification and a general depreciation of inter-personal relationships. Humor is in the service of manipulating the environment. He knows what one is expected to feel guilty about but does not experience a sense of guilt. Violence is taken lightly, without appreciation of its meaning. The protocol is pervaded by psychopathic elements. Fantasy is used for withdrawal and wish-gratification, and as a preconscious planning device for manipulation. The life he leads is one of *isolation and lacks meaningful relationships*.

Summary: Psychological testing of a group of former patients diagnosed as borderline supports the diagnosis in all essential points and corroborates the characteristics of the subgroups established by Grinker et al. for the syndrome. Except for one doubtful case, no movement from one subgroup to another over the intervening years has occurred. Structural defects of the ego are present and there is evidence of early disturbances in object relations and tenuous impulse control.

In general, Gunderson and Singer's (1975) review of the psychological literature confirms Gruenewald's findings. They state that the borderline patient does well on the structured WAIS test, but less well on the unstructured Rorschach. The available psychological reports on the fourteen new cases are presented in chapter 3 with the individual case protocols (cases 9, 11, 12, 13, 14, 18, and 19).

Chapter 7
Follow-Up Studies

Clinical diagnoses are incomplete when they are limited to the observations and descriptions of symptoms, behaviors, or functions at one time. The natural history of disease is important, and the longitudinal course and outcome of any entity are necessary data for a comprehensive diagnosis. In our original research design we obtained descriptions of our patients' behaviors about two weeks after admission and again later, when discharge from the hospital was imminent. The data from this second period were not very different from those from the first.

We therefore decided, after our primary study had been completed, to follow our patients and ascertain their subsequent status. A further reason for the follow-up study involved our curiosity regarding the effect of treatment during hospitalization. The treatment program can be described as belonging to the vague category *milieu therapy*. This entails a warm and accepting climate, yet one structured by limits. It includes demonstrations of reality-oriented behavior on the part of the staff. There are weekly activity, action, and planning meetings, many informal patient groups, formal group therapy involving four to eight patients at a time, and a group which prepares the patients for discharge.

The staff were specifically interrogated about the future of the study patients: "Will he make it?" The basis for prognosis used by the staff and the director of the unit is the same and holds for patients of all types. If the patient can talk about his feelings and problems, look honestly at his own behavior, and survey the resources abailable to him, the prognosis is good. If he does not involve himself in the milieu program but instead engages in denial of his problems and withdraws, the prognosis is poor.

The final reason for the follow-up study was to determine whether the outcome differentiated the groups in the criterion sample of patients and in the sample of patients who dropped out. Thus we followed the fifty-one criterion patients who had remained in the hospital on the open research nursing unit for the time required to obtain two observational periods. We also undertook to follow the seventeen patients who were lost to the study due to transfer, elopement, on discharge against medical advice, or whose behavior required the use of large doses of tranquilizing drugs.

Our first approach to the study subjects was a letter, written by the director of the hospital on official hospital stationery, indicating our interest in how they were doing and suggesting that an appointment be made by telephone with a part-time assistant assigned to interview the subjects. When subjects did not respond to the letter in a reasonable time, we attempted to establish contact with them by telephone. Not more than six letters were mailed at one time to avoid long-time lags between the initial letter and our follow-up telephone call. Dealing with a small number at a time facilitated reaching subjects and setting appointments flexibly.

We obtained data on forty-four of the fifty-one patients in our criterion group, forty-one of whom were living in the community at the time of follow-up. The seven subjects for whom we do not have follow-up data had moved and could not be traced. We attempted to find out if these seven differed in any way from the others. Actually two fell in each of Groups I and III, three in Group II, and none in Group IV; thus they occupied almost the whole range of the borderline. Without going into detail, we can summarize by stating that to greater or lesser degrees they fit the borderline syndrome and displayed no social characteristics that differed markedly from the group as a whole.

We defined social functioning, the major content of our follow-up, as the individual's adaptation to his responsibilities and his relationships with people. We did not attempt to assess the extent of psychopathology at follow-up. Social functioning was the information sought, on the assumption that the recovery level of the former psychiatric patient is reflected by the adequacy of his social adjustment. The follow-up interviews investigated not only the current functioning of subjects but also the course of their experiences between discharge and follow-up and the major modifications that took place with reference to living arrangements, use of leisure time, relations to family, friends, and co-workers, marital status, children, employment, education, and posthospital psychiatric care. We attempted to assess not only the factual picture of social functioning but also the subjects' satisfaction with their own functioning.

Perhaps a second criterion is more important that the ability to stay out of the hospital—the former patient's performance as a community member. Residence in the community and participation in its activities are accorded high value in our society. Adequate occupational and social performance is at least one of the ways that the healthy and sick are differentiated. Well people work, and sick people must work to become well.

Occupational Adjustments

The role most generally expected of adults in our society is probably instrumental performance with reference to work. For adult men this usually means regular employment in a gainful occupation, and for adult women either gainful employment or responsible management of homemaking activities.

The extent to which our subjects fulfilled their social roles occupationally was measured by a five-point work-performance scale modified from Adler (1955). A score of 5 was assigned to the best performance and a score of 1 to those unable to work at all. Fifty-four percent of the forty-one found in the community on follow-up were performing occupationally at the two top levels.

Work Regularity Between Discharge and Follow-up
(Classified on a 5-Point Scale)

	Male	Female	Total	Percent
Total	23	18	41	100
Score				
5 Regularly employed, regularly attending school, or both employed and attending school If housewife, managing household alone	11	8	19	47
4 Frequent job change without substantial periods of unemployment	3		3	7
3 With substantial periods of unemployment	5	4	9	22
2 Employed occasionally	1	4	5	12
1 Employed not at all	3	2	5	12

At the time of their admission to the hospital less than one third of the patients were employed in white-collar occupations and had at least completed high school. Most performed in occupational roles that required only limited interaction with people and limited initiative. *From admission to follow-up there were no changes in the general level of their educational and occupational status and consequently in the amount of interaction and initiative required of them in their work.*

Educationally these patients were predominantly a group of school dropouts. Thirty-seven percent had entered but not completed college; 29 percent had entered but not completed high school. At follow-up four were attending night school with the aim of earning a college degree. At follow-up the median age of the males was about twenty-five years; the females thirty years. All in all, movement upward occupationally could not be expected of these people. The facts suggest that, although gainfully employed and largely self-sufficient economically, the group was occupationally and academically static at a fairly low level.

A five-point scale based on the one originated by Adler (1955) was used to measure social participation. On this scale, we measured the use of leisure time and the extent of contact with friends and people other than the family with whom the patient lived. We were forced to use this dimension alone, since there was no evidence that these patients participated in voluntary associations or in any of the activities of the larger community.

Our findings suggest gross deficiencies in their social relations and use of leisure time. Only 17 percent were found at the two upper levels. The modal group is described by limited leisure-time activities involving transient contact with people. At the two lower points on the scale the patients live in virtual isolation. One can only conclude from these results that the strong emphasis in the milieu therapy program on developing skills in interpersonal relations did not carry over into the community lives of these subjects. Although more than half of the total group had had transient posthospital contact with their former fellow patients, few sustained this contact over time. There was no evidence of deep and abiding relationships

Social Participation of Former Patients Based on Use of Leisure Time and Contact with People

	Male	Female	Total	Percent
Total in Community	23	18	41	100
Score				
5 Very active social life involving much contact with people	2	4	6	15
4 Active social life involving contact with people	1		1	2
3 Leisure-time activities limited, involving transient contact with people	8	7	15	36
2 No leisure-time activities, evidence of minimal social contact with people	8	5	13	32
1 No leisure-time activities, no friends, and no evidence of social contact with people	8	5	13	32

formed from their hospital experience. One can infer that social participation constitutes a more problematic area of adjustment for this group than occupation, since there is no involvement in formal social activities and very little in informal social activities.

Family Relations

Males and females of the same age at the time of follow-up differed significantly with respect to marital status. Less than 30 percent of the females but 70 percent of the males had never married. Although the marital status of males and females differed significantly within our group, the incidence of single, never married persons of both sexes is higher in our group than in the general population of the same age in the Chicago area (according to the 1960 census).

Marital Status at Follow-up

	Male	Female	Total
Total	23	18	41
Ever Married	7	13	20
Married to same spouse as during hospital stay	3	1	4
Married since discharge		3	3
Remarried since discharge		3	3
Divorced prior to hospital stay		2	2
Divorced since discharge	1	2	3
Separated	3	2	5
Single, Never Married	16	5	21

The majority of the subjects were living in a family setting, defined as a household, containing either a parent, spouse, child, or cousin. The unattached males most often lived with their parents, the females with spouse and/or children. Only nine of the total group were living alone. But between discharge and follow-up, the group had not necessarily been residentially stable. Some of the single males tried to live alone in various places before settling down with their parents.

Living Arrangements at Follow-up of 41 Patients
Living in the Community

Living Arrangements	Number of Patients			
	Male	Female	Total	Percent
Total	23	18	41	100
With family	18	14	32	78
With one or both parents	14	3	17	
With spouse	3	7	10	
With children	—	3	3	
Other	1	1	2	
Alone	5	4	9	22

Relations to family were coded on two bases: (1) how well the subject claimed he was getting along with spouse, children, and/or parents; (2) the emotional strains the subject experienced in getting along.

Relations to family were coded on two bases: (1) how well the subject claimed he was getting along with spouse, children, and/or parents; (2) the emotional strains the subject experienced in getting along.

Family Adjustment Scores

	Male	Female	Total	Percent
Total	23	18	41	100

Score

5 Gets along well with central family figures; more comfortable with a formerly conflictual relation

	1	5	6	15

4 Gets along with central family figures but expresses some emotional strain

	6	2	8	19

Patient's Assessment of His Psychological State

		Male	Female	Total	Percent
	Total	23	18	41	100
Score					
3	Feels well; expresses improvement	2	4	6	15
2	Feels better; expresses qualifications	4	4	8	19
1	Feels some change, but considerable qualification	12	2	14	34
0	Feels no change or worse	5	8	13	32

even worse. If we take the subject's assessment of his psychological condition as given, we can conclude that self-perception is an ego-strength of these people. Few of them reported either the use of drugs (6) or excessive use of alcohol (4); only one subject reported smoking marijuana. It is surprising, in view of their conservative estimates of their psychological well-being, that relatively few were resorting to drugs and alcohol.

Relation of Predictions to Follow-up

As mentioned early in this chapter, we obtained a set of separate concluding summary ratings on every patient, labeled *Synthesis*. One of the questions on the form concerned the patient's capacity for problem solving assessed along five dimensions:

Delays action appropriately in pursuit of solutions to problems

Family Adjustment Scores (continued)

	Male	Female	Total
3 Managing to get along; emotional strain present but not serious	5	2	7
2 Expresses serious reservation about relations with central family figures	5	1	6
1 Does not get along, isolated, little or no contact	6	8	1⸱

Nearly one half of the subjects experienced seriou‹ tions about their relations to central family figur‹ isolated from their families. The unattached male‹ gravitate toward their parental homes, which may ⸱ the frequency of the claims that they were gettin‹ were managing to get along with their famili‹ serious strain. The stresses of living with parent‹ tolerated, or they would have been forced to ad‹ way of life.

Subject's Estimate of his Psychological Health

We asked the subject about his view of his p‹ health. If he claimed to feel better since dischar‹ him to specify the improvements; if worse, to setbacks. In this manner we obtained the pluses of the subject's self-assessment of his psychologi‹

The subjects were modest and seldom ‹ unqualified state of well-being. Sixty-six perc‹ considerable qualification or claimed they wer‹

2. Weighs and selects among the demands of social pressures and influences
3. Applies his thoughts to a problem
4. Foresees consequences of decisions and actions
5. Chooses realistically among alternative courses of action

A second question required a prediction: "To what degree is the patient able to carry on his usual life processes?" The ratings on these two questions—"problem solving capacity" and "capacity to carry on usual life processes"—were assessed on the basis of the protocols of the behavior of the patients observed during their hospital stay. Ratings were made on a four-point scale, ranging zero, low, moderate, and high. When the predictive ratings were related to the total overall assessment scores, it was found that the mean follow-up scores for those who were rated zero and low and those rated moderate and high on capacity to carry on usual life processes differed significantly in the expected direction. We may conclude that the predictions were supported by the follow-up.

Summary

The follow-up study provided data which enlarge and amplify our picture of the borderline as a diagnostic entity. The follow-up as an external criterion provides at least moderate evidence of patient group differentiation. Any improvement in one way or another in our sample at follow-up was not associated with improved adaptation to the community or better skill in interpersonal relations. Milieu therapy did not carry over strongly into the lives of these patients in the community. *They remained socially awkward.*

In 1970, Werble reported a second follow-up of the forty-four patients who had responded to the first follow-up study. This study was conducted for the purpose of adding to our understanding of the natural history of the syndrome, its longitudinal course, and its outcome. Did they deteriorate or improve? Did they become overtly schizophrenic, as some skeptical critics had predicted?

In contrast to the first follow-up only twenty-eight patients responded. The attrition rate is always considerable among a sample of psychiatric patients, but we had neither the time nor the patience to extend our tedious original research to more patients. Without going into the numbers or percentages outlined in our monograph and in Werble's 1970 paper, we may summarize the current findings.

As with most people who have reached their late twenties and early thirties, the life styles of our twenty-eight subjects are well established. Since 1965 there has been little individual change in their social functioning. Slight undulations do occur in the lives of some, for instance, a woman whose separated husband returns to her responds positively with some evidence of improved, though not qualitatively different, social functioning. The stability in the life styles of the group is confirmed by the steady picture of employment they present. Awareness of their own traits can be counted an ego-strength. With few exceptions, adaptations are made within very constricted limits. Since a repertory of roles is not available to these people, whatever stable equilibrium they achieve is very costly. There are very few human object relations in their lives. We cannot predict what will happen to them when these few objects pass from the scene. These former patients gave no evidence in their social functioning of movement toward schizophrenia.

Additional information serving as a sort of second follow-up may be found in Gruenewald's 1970 paper, which was derived from psychological studies of ten original cases, although only three were presented in detail. None of the three were schizophrenic—all corresponded, in psychological language of course, to our clinical descriptions of the borderline "early disturbances in object relations and tenuous impulse control."

Currently we have attempted to extend our follow-up study of the twenty-eight patients who were available for the 1970 report. This time (probably the last) only ten responded. Three were in Group III, two in Group I, and one in Group IV. Briefly stated, the female in Group IV is married, has three children, is sociable and enjoys life. Those in Group I are single, can't make friends, have little energy, and have periods of isolation. Those in Group III are about the same, with no close friends and just about getting by.

We would assume that this follow-up is skewed toward the more adaptive responding rather than toward those in trouble or requiring rehospitalization because of alcoholism, drug abuse, or angry asocial attacks. But as far as we know none are schizophrenic. A further statement of follow-up of 1976 cases is too sparse to use as a criterion. A statement of their status follows the individual case reports (chapter 3).

Chapter 8
Stable Instability

The original goal of our research, as stated in *The Borderline Syndrome*, was to define the psychiatric entity frequently referred to as *borderline*. This term in itself has many historical and contemporary meanings. Although attempts have been made by a number of individual therapists to allocate this diagnosis to a specific syndrome, in general it has been used as a depository for any clinical uncertainty. Even this usage is not specific because the same uncertainty existing in many clinics is hidden by the use of at least a dozen terms, ranging from chronic undifferentiated schizophrenia to personality character neuroses. These special terms seem to designate commonalities of visible symptoms rather than patterns of functions or dysfunctions. Our attempt to define what it denotes as a clinical psychiatric syndrome is confusing to those who expect the definition to include literally what borders on what. We have given much consideration to developing a new diagnostic appellation, but this seems almost impossible in view of the long use of the old one and despite the fact it remains semantically unclear.

Our primary goal, then, was to determine whether a borderline syndrome exists and, if so, what its attributes are. Second, we hoped to ascertain if subcategories could be delineated and, if so, to define them. Thus the goal at the onset of the research was to answer the question, What is the borderline? Finally, in this volume we wished to describe individual patients so that the clincial psychiatrist could more easily diagnose his own patients and thereby know their prognosis and appropriate treatment, if any.

We began our investigations in an era when clinical diagnoses and classifications were derogated, diagnostic skills atrophied, and the life history of psychiatic entities of no great concern. These tendencies were self-perpetuating, because students were taught to focus, sometimes exclusively, on the internal dynamics of individual patients.

Our overview of an extensive professional literature, although selective, disclosed that no systematic study of the borderline had ever been made. The same lack was found as regards other diagnostic terms serving the purpose of labeling vague syndromes. The bulk of published reports were based on one patient or a few for whom treatment represented the only method of observation.

Despite these criticisms, which are more general than specific and applicable to a whole specialty, the positive contributions suggested that the borderline is a specific syndrome with considerable degree of internal consistency and stability, and not a regression in response to internal or external conditions of stress. It represents a syndrome characteristic of arrested development of ego-functions. Clinicians have recognized that the borderline syndrome is a confusing combination of psychotic, neurotic, and character disturbances with many normal or healthy elements. Although these symptoms are unstable, the syndrome itself as a *process* is recognizably stable, giving rise to the peculiar term *stable instability*.

We decided to study the ego processes of borderline patients insofar as they are exposed by ongoing behaviors. Using an ego-psychology framework promised a better understanding of the syndrome and its subcategories. Our research design was based, therefore, on a specifc approach: in essence we observed and described behaviors and then rated traits extracted from ego psychology. This extraction required the redefinition of ego-functions into behavioral variables as exactly as possible.

In our design we could not include all hypothesized ego-functions since many are not expressed in behavior; others which were included had to be dropped because of insufficient evidence. Some qualities of the borderline patient could not be evoked and in fact may have been inhibited by the nonstressful characteristics of the hospital nursing unit. The behaviors that we did observe were linked to the specificity of the environment within which they occurred—far less stressful than the real world. Even the decision for discharge and the planning for posthospital living and work, which we intended for our second period of "observation-description-rating" was not stressful, probably because borderline patients do not become committed to the institution. Their reluctance to leave was based on a distaste for living away from their families or for taking jobs requiring contact with people.

In the present volume we have studied fourteen new borderline patients who appeared in our current schizophrenic research program. They were not preselected, in Gunderson's words (1975), as if we had "packed a suitcase." Rather, we interviewed, rated, diagnosed, and followed up a sample of young adults between seventeen and twenty-eight years of age as they were consecutively admitted to the hospital. The interviewer and the raters did not know the admitting diagnosis nor the diagnoses made during the course of hospitalization. The nonschizophrenics serve as a control for the schizophrenics, the primary focus of research at this time. Fourteen borderline patients were found and these are described in some detail, some with psychological test material.

The four groups elicited by our statistical analysis when translated into clinical syndromes coincide with clinical experience. In general, Group I is closest to the psychotic border, Group IV to the neurotic; Group II represents the core process of the borderline, and Group III is the most adaptive. compliant, and lacking in identity ("as if").

In defining the overall characteristics of the borderline syndrome we include (1) anger as the main or only affect, (2) defect in affectional relationships, (3) an absence of indications of self-identity, and (4) depressive loneliness.

Within this gestalt the various groups represent different positions. Members of Group I give up attempts at relationship but at the same time overtly, in behavior and affect, react negatively and angrily toward other people and to their environment. Persons in Group II are inconsistent, moving toward others for relations followed by acted-out repulsion and a moving away into isolation, where they are lonely and depressed. This back-and-forth movement is characteristic and corresponds to the fact that these people are both angry and depressed, but at different times. Patients in Group III seem to have given up their search for identity and defend against their reactions to an empty world. They do not have the angry reactions characteristic of Group I. Instead they passively await cues from others and behave in complementarity—"as if." In no other group were the defenses observable as clearly or as consistently as in Group III. Subjects in Group IV serach for a lost symbiotic relation with a mother figure which they do not achieve or maintain, and then reveal what may be called an anclitic depression.

Groups I and III showed an affinity, as did Groups II and IV. This makes clinical sense because patients in both Groups I and III have given up hope of meaningful relationships and those in Groups II and IV are still searching. Patients in Group I are angry at the world and their ego integrations are endangered by this strong affect; we hypothesize that as a result they often become temporarily psychotic. Those in Group III have given up even their reactions to frustration and are compliant, passive, and relate as others wish; they successfully defend themselves against angry behavior and eruptions.

Group II includes patients who are buffeted by their own ego-dysfunctions as they attempt to relate to others, become stimulated to anger, and then withdraw and suffer loneliness. Group IV, on the other hand, comprises patients characterized by abandonment of any but dependent clinging relationships; when these are not gratified, the patients' develop the characteristics of an anaclitic depression, weeping and feeling neglected and sorry for themselves.

The next step, after the characteristic behavioral traits of the borderline category, its subgroups and factors had been put together, was to check them against total case reports of individual patients. We used the protocols of our fifty-one patients, an in-depth study of sixteen additional patients who comprised an experimental group previously studied, and several patients who were in treatment at the time. In this volume, as stated above, we have added individual descriptions of fourteen new borderline patients and a section on differential diagnosis. Using the behavioral characteristics of each of the four groups isolated by statistical methods, we were able to place all the patients in appropriate groups. Thus the statistical differentiation of the whole syndrome and of the four groups made logical clinical sense.

Clinically we need to differentiate the core of the borderline process from such peripheral symptoms as drug abuse, suicide, anorexia, and asocial behavior. These peripheral symptoms may appear in almost any of the mental disorders—neuroses, personality disorders, psychoses—and even in normals. The diagnosis of the boderline is made on the manifestations of the core processes italicized in the clinical profiles. Thus the peripheral symptoms are not concerned with the central process of the borderline, although there are "explanations" for them. Furthermore, as would be expected, there are some evidences of overlap among the four groups, although the core process of each is clealy identifiable.

Interest has shifted from specific mother-child relations as primary causes in the development of neuroses and psychoses, to the family of origin. Viewed as a system in its own right and not simply as a collection of individuals, the family has caused investigators to search for its methods of interaction and problem solving, and especially its modes of communication. The literature contains significant references to disturbed communication systems in families of schizophrenics, but none specific to the borderline.

Since the study of the family was not included in our original research design, we were forced to use social service data rated according to specific criteria by an independent rater. Although the families of the borderline patients showed the usual range of concern about the illness, no specific type of family was correlated with any of the borderline groups. Nevertheless a by-product of this study was a technique for family analysis which discriminated family types (chapter 5). As for the individual borderline patient, he marries infrequently and is an inadequate spouse and parent.

To obtain a perspective on the borderline over time, we conducted a follow-up study. We were highly successful in interviewing the majority of our residual first patient sample (86 percent) and about 40 percent of the dropouts. Essentially we found that borderline patients in the time from one to three and a half years after hospitalization, did not, with the exception of two patients in Group I, become schizophrenic. Despite a type of learning therapy administered in the hospital and oriented toward improving the social aptitudes of the patients, they remained for the most part socially isolated. Yet most of those with some psychiatric contacts returned to school or employment and maintained their instrumental roles successfully. Thirteen patients had to be rehospitalized, five of whom had been hospitalized more than once before. Of the dropouts, only one turned out to be borderline.

Subsequent follow-up studies five years later (Werble 1970) revealed a high attrition rate. Only twenty-eight of the original patients could be found after a vigorous search. This follow-up also revealed that these patients maintained their position and did not become schizophrenic. This year, ten years later, follow-up contributed only seven patients who responded. Although small in number, they too had remained as they were, with no shifting from one group to another. Reference should be made to Helene Deutsch's twenty-five-year follow-up of several of her "as if" type of borderline cases, none of whom showed any change in their core processes.

We have to surmise that, as in any follow-up study, those who cooperated and furnished information were more stable and better off psychologically than those not responding. Possibly those who were "lost" had fled to an easier environment to which they could adapt, that is, had found a more suitable ecological niche. Although our patients in Group IV are few and mostly female, it seems that marriage to a "motherly husband" who can tolerate periodic withdrawals in his borderline spouse results in a relatively stable life for such women. Those among the follow-up respondents who are most successful seem to have developed a searching introspection into their difficulties and to have learned how to adapt.

We cannot discuss the treatment of the borderline patient from our personal experience after 1968; however, we have followed up many of the old and new patients and know that they remain socially awkward and have considerable difficulty in "object relations." No one is cured, which could not be expected since developmental defect stems from the early stage of separation-individuation and has left a profound disturbance in their identities. They apparently cannot utilize the repressive defenses of the neurotic, yet neither do they have the impaired reality testing of the schizophrenic. Aside from their identity diffusion, they suffer from an inability to attain and maintain positive object relations. Thus they require direction, control, and education rather than insight, since they do not have the capacity to develop a transference neurosis suitable for psychoanalytic interpretations.

A recent suggestion by Klein (1975) is to use specific drugs for the various subtypes of the borderline. The core type profits from Thorazine and lithium, another group has a high degree of thyroid deficiency, and those with panic attacks profit from Valium. The specificity of such drugs requires much further study, but there is no question that drugs, like other, more psychological techniques, are valuable in the treatment of symptoms rather than as curative procedures.

Posing the question, How does a human being become a borderline?—in other words, attempting to determine the etiology of the syndrome—makes us realize how little information we have to draw on. It has been easy, but of little value, for writers to discuss deficiences in early child-mother relations, or neglectful mothering, or even infantile traumata. Discussions of genic, familial, and general environmental aspects of etiology have been equally vague.

That many factors are involved in the ontogenesis of personality, "normality," and illness is an twentieth-century conclusion opposed by several schools of psychiatry, which contend they possess all the information necessary for causal explanation and therapy. Against such ideologies a reactionary interest in "unified" and global theories of human behavior sometimes called "holistic," "biopsychosical," or "general systems theory" has developed.

Unfortunately, global theories are abstractions so far removed from experimental and empirical data that they have no external referents and serve only as umbrellas for other subtheories. Yet they are fruitful in that they attempt to connect in some fashion the several levels of discourse characteristic of the subtheories, and to bring within the boundaries of real or conceptual systems behaviors of many types as viewed by appropriate disciplines.

The borderline personality becomes crystallized as a style of life from its system variants. But which aspects of experience are relevant to this crystallization—the kinds of people and situations that catalyze it—this is as yet a matter of pure conjecture. We cannot determine where and when the developmental defect occurs, nor even whether it is biogenetic or psychogenetic. Signs of the process may occur early or late, depending on external events. The borderline personality may shift into the overt syndrome and become irreversible, but we do not know the precipitating causes of this shift. Then again, favorable life situations or treatment may result in a remission into a borderline personality status, even on a permanent basis.

The influence of genic or constitutional qualities as well as the effect of society and culture in general continue throughout life. Constitution and society act as restraining walls to an otherwise open system with reverberating transactions penetrating the individual's boundaries from both directions. In behavior (action or reaction) or in defensive maneuvers, the human being is limited by his genic physical constitution, the speed and quality of his neurological functions, his intelligence and special talents. What he is born with imposes limitations on his behavior. Likewise the general culture of his social environment imposes limitations on his deviance from the general order. Should he transgress these restrictions he moves from being merely different or eccentric to becoming criminally or psychotically aberrant, at which point he is consigned to prison or hospital.

Within the parts of the borderline system, and even more clearly in the borderline personality, are the components of his life style. These encompass not only his usual behavior but also his stress responses to stimuli that strain his integrative capacities. Initial defenses may take the form of such internal shifts in functional organization as compensation of one function for another or acceleration or slowing of communication. In reaction to stimuli which cannot be handled internally, the response is generalized and manifested in overt behavior. It is then that the characteristic withdrawal and denial or, obversely, the angry attack on others occurs. Finally, anxiety may mount and the individual, suffering the impact of outer stimuli and flooded with rage from within, becomes temporarily confused and is labeled psychotic.

It matters little whether we call the borderline syndrome a disease, an arrest of development, an emotional disturbance, or a type of behavioral deviance. Likewise it is restrictive to view the borderline from a single frame of reference such as the biological, medical, psychological, or social. The borderline, like health and illness, is a system in process occurring in time: developing, progressing, and regressing as a focus of a large biopsychosocial field.

References

Ackerman, N. (1958). *The Psychodynamics of Family Life.* New York: Basic Books.

Adler, L. M. (1955). Patients of a state mental hospital: the outcome of their hospitalization. In *Mental Health and Mental Disorder*, ed. A. Rose, pp. 501-523. New York: Norton.

Artiss, K. L. (1966). Language and the schizophrenic quandary. *Contemporary Psychoanalysis* 3:39-54.

Beck, S. J. (1964). Symptom and trait in schizophrenia. *American Journal of Orthopsychiatry* 34:517-526.

Bentley, A. F. (1950). Kennetic inquiry. *Science* 112:775-777.

Birdwhistell, R. L. (1966). The American family. *Psychiatry* 29:204-212.

Bleuler, E. (1950). *Dementia Praecox or the Group of Schizophrenics.* Trans. J. Zinkin. Monograph Series in Schizophrenia No. 1. New York: International Universities Press.

Bleuler, E. (1955). *Lehrbuch der Psychiatrie.* 9th ed. Ed. M. Bleuler. Berlin: Springer.

Bychowski, G. (1957). Psychic structure and therapy of latent schizophrenia. In *Schizophrenia in Psychoanalytic Office Practice*, ed. A. Rifkin. New York: Grune and Stratton.

Clark, L. P. (1919). Some practical remarks upon the use of modified psychoanalysis in the treatment of borderline (borderland) neuroses and psychoses. *Psychoanalytic Review* 6:306-315.

Deutsch, H. (1942). Some forms of emotional disturbances and their relationship to schizophrenia. *Psychoanalytic Quarterly* 11:301-321.

Dickes, Robert (1974). The concepts of borderline states: an alternative proposal. *International Journal of Psychoanalytic Psychotherapy* 3:1-27.

Dyrud, Jarl E. (1972). The treatment of the borderline syndrome. In *Modern Psychiatry and Clinical Research*, ed. Offer, Daniel and Freedman, Daniel, pp. 159-173. New York: Basic Books.

Eisenstein, W. W. (1952). Differential psychotherapy of borderline states. In *Specialized Techniques in Psychotherapy*, ed. G. Bychowski and J.L. Despert. New York: Basic Books.

Ekstein, R. and Wallerstein, J. (1954). Observations on the psychology of borderline and psychotic children. *Psychoanalytic Study of the Child* 9:344-369.

Federn, P. (1952). *Ego Psychology and the Psychoses.* New York: Basic Books.

Fenichel, O. (1945). *The Psychoanalytic Theory of the Neuroses.* New York: Norton.

Fleck, S. (1966). An approach to family pathology. *Comprehensive Psychiatry* 7:307-320.

Fried, E. (1956). Ego strengthening aspects of hostility. *American Journal of Orthopsychiatry* 26:179-187.

Frosch, J. (1964). The psychotic character, clinical psychiatric consideration. *Psychiatric Quarterly* 39:81-96.

Glover, E. (1932). Psychoanalytic approach to the classification of mental disorders. *Journal of Mental Science* 78:819-842.

Goldfarb, W. (1955). Emotional and intellectual consequences of psychological deprivation in infancy. In *Psychopathology of Childhood*, ed. P. H. Hoch and J. Zubin. New York: Grune and Stratton.

Grinker, R. R., Sr. (1964). Psychiatry rides madly in all directions. *Archives of General Psychiatry* 10:228-237.

Grinker, R. R., Sr., Miller, J., Sabshin, M., Nunn, R., and Nunnally, J. C. (1961). *The Phenomena of Depressions.* New York: Hoeber.

Grinker, R. R., Sr., Werble, B., and Drye, R. (1968). *The Borderline Syndrome.* New York: Basic Books.

Groves, James E. (1975). Management of the borderline patient on a medical or surgical ward: the psychiatric consultant's role. *International Journal of Psychiatry in Medicine* 6:337-348.

Gruenewald, D. (1970). A psychologist's view of the borderline syndrome. *Archives of General Psychiatry* 23:180-184.

Gunderson, John G., Carpenter, William T., and Strauss, John S. (1975). Borderline and schizophrenic patients: a comparative study. *American Journal of Psychiatry* 132:1257-1264.

Gunderson, John G., and Singer, Margaret T. (1975). Defining borderline patients: an overview. *American Journal of Psychiatry* 132:1-10.

Guze, S. B. (1975). Differential diagnosis of the borderline. In *Borderline States in Psychiatry*, ed. J. Mack. New York: Grune and Stratton.

Hoch, P. H. (1963). Personal communication to Roy R. Grinker, Sr., February 7.

Hoch, P. H. (1972). *Differential Diagnosis in Clinical Psychiatry*. New York: Jason Aronson.

Hoch, P. H., and Cattell, J. (1959). The diagnosis of pseudoneurotic schizophrenia. *Psychiatric Quarterly* 33:17-43.

Hoch, P. H., and Polatin, P. (1949). Pseudoneurotic forms of schizophrenia. *Psychiatric Quarterly* 23:248-276.

Hughes, C. (1884). Borderline psychiatric records: pro-dromal symptoms of physical impairments. *Alienist and Neurologist* 5:85-90.

Jones, W. A. (1918). Borderland cases, mental and nervous. *Lancet*, n.s. 38:561-567.

Kernberg, Otto (1967). Borderline personality organization. *Journal of the American Psychoanalytic Association* 15:641-685.

Kernberg, Otto (1968). The treatment of patients with borderline personality organization. *International Journal of Psycho-Analysis* 49:600-619.

Kety, Seymour S., Rosenthal, David, Wender, Paul H., and Schulsinger, Fini (1971). Mental illness in the biological and adoptive schizophrenics. *American Journal of Psychiatry* 128:302-306.

Klein, D. F. (1975). Psychopharmacology and the borderline patient. In *Borderline States in Psychiatry*, ed. J. Mack. New York: Grune and Stratton.

Knight, R. P. ed. (1953). Borderline states. In *Drives, Affects, Behavior*, ed. R. Loewenstein. pp. 203-215. International Universities Press.

———, ed. (1954). Borderline states. In *Psychoanalytic Psychiatry and Psychology*. New York: International Universities Press.

Kraepelin, E. (1912). *Clinical Psychiatry*. 7th ed. Trans. A. R. Diefendort. New York: Macmillan.

Lidz, T., Fleck, S., and Cornelison, A. R. (1965). *Schizophrenia and the Family*. New York: International Universities Press.

Mack, John E., ed. (1975). *Borderline States in Psychiatry*. New York: Grune and Stratton.

Maddi, S. R. (1968). *Personality Theories, A Comparative Analysis*. Homewood, Illinois: Dorsey Press.

Masterson, J. F. (1976). *Psychotherapy of the Borderline Adult*. New York: Brunner-Mazel.

Menninger, K. (1963). *The Vital Balance*. New York: Viking.

Mischler, E., and Waxler, N. (1966). Family interaction processes and schizophrenia. *International Journal of Psychiatry* 2:375-428.

Modell, A. H. (1963). Primitive object relationship and predisposition to schizophrenia. *International Journal of Psycho-Analysis* 44:282-292.

Oken, D., Grinker, R. R., Sr., Heath, H. A., Sabshin, M., and Schwartz, N. (1960). Stress response in a group of chronic psychiatric patients. *Archives of General Psychiatry* 3:45-46.

Parkin, A. (1966). Neuroses and psychoses: I. Historical review: II. Modern Perspective. *Psychiatric Quarterly* 40:203-227.

Perry, Christopher J., and Klerman, Gerald L. Prepublication Manuscript. The borderline patient: a comparative analysis of four sets of diagnostic criteria.

Pfeiffer, Eric (1974). Borderline states. *Diseases of the Nervous System* 35:212-219.

Rosenfeld, S. K., and Sprince, M. P. (1963). Some thoughts on the technical handling of borderline children. *Psychoanalytic Study of the Child* 20:495-517.

Rosse, J.C. (1890). Clinical evidence of borderline insanity. *Journal of Nervous and Mental Diseases* 17:669-674.

Schmideberg, M. (1959). The borderline patient. In *American Handbook of Psychiatry*, vol. 1, ed. S. Arieti, pp. 398-418. New York: Basic Books.

Shakow, D. (1971). Some observations on the psychology (and some fewer on the biology) of schizophrenia. *Journal of Nervous and Mental Diseases* 153:300-316.

Stengel, E. (1959). Classification of mental disorders. *Bulletin of the World Health Organization* 21:601-663.

Stern, A. (1938). Psychoanalytic investigation of and therapy in the borderline group of neuroses. *Psychoanalytic Quarterly* 7:467-489.

Waelder, R. (1960). *Basic Theories of Psychoanalysis*. New York: International Universities Press.

Weingarten, L. L., and Korn, S. (1967). Psychological test findings on pseudoneurotic schizophrenics. *Archives of General Psychiatry* 17:448-454.

Weiss, J. (1966). Reporter: Clinical and theoretical aspects of the "as if" characters (Participants: Atkin, Tartakoff, Ross, Greenson, Katan, Deutsch, Chase, Bychowsky, Kaywin). *Journal of the American Psychoanalytic Association* 14:569-591.

Wender, P. (1968). In *The Transmission of Schizophrenia*, ed. D. Rosenthal and S. Kety. New York: Pergamon Press.

Werble, B. (1970) Second follow-up of borderline patients. *Archives of General Psychiatry* 23:3-7.

Wolberg, A. (1952). The borderline patient. *American Journal of Psychotherapy* 6:694-701.

Wynne, L. C., and Singer, M. T. (1963). Thought disorder and family relations of schizophrenics. *Archives of General Psychiatry* 9:199-206.

Zuk, G. H., and Boszormenyi-Nagy, I. (1967). *Family Therapy and Disturbed Families*. Palo Alto, California: Science and Behavior Books.

Index